AIR FRYER COOKBOOK

QUICK AND EASY LOW CARB AIR FRYER RECIPES TO
LOSE WEIGHT, BAKE, FRY, ROAST AND GRILL.

FRANCESCA BONHEUR

APEX UNIVERSAL PTY LTD

CONTENTS

Book Description: About This Book
Introduction

1. Air Fryer Breakfast Recipes

Nutritional information
Cinnamon Almond Toast
Gluten Free Ham Frittata
Granola with chocolate and Hazelnuts
Avocado Egg Boats
Cloud pancakes with scallions
Whole wheat Burritos
Air Fried pancakes
Air Fried pancakes

2. Lunch Recipes

Crispy Chicken Livers
Chicken with broccoli and sesame
Chicken with sesame and Orange sauce
Chicken with Parmesan cheese
Turkey breast with thyme and sage
Chicken Pizza
Almond Crusted Chicken
Pistachio stuffed chicken
Chicken balls with tomato sauce
Beef Rouladen
Beef meat Jerky
Vegan Lasagna
Air Fried white fish with nuts
Shrimps with oregano and pepper flakes
Air fried salmon with herbs
Codfish with Lemon Juice
Fish Nuggets with lemon juice

3. Side Dishes

Potato Chips with Rosemary
Zucchini Patties with Parmesan cheese
Chicken Chipotle
Cauliflower bites

4. Snacks And Appetizers

Samosa with potatoes and peas
Tomatoes with Herbs
Stuffed peppers with ground turkey

5. Dessert Recipes

Macadamia cookies
Macaroons with Pistachio topping
Chocolate Bars
Orange Cake
Almond Semolina cake
Crispy Low carb glazed pastry dessert
Crunchy Walnut cookies
Raspberry coconut balls
Glazed Donuts

6. Recipe Index

7. Conclusion

Thank you for Reading This Book
Also by Francesca Bonheur
About the Author

༓ Copyright 2017 Francesca Bonheur - All rights reserved.

This document is geared towards providing exact and reliable information in regards to the topic and issue covered. The publication is sold with the idea that the publisher is not required to render accounting, officially permitted, or otherwise, qualified services. If advice is necessary, legal or professional, a practiced individual in the profession should be ordered.

- From a Declaration of Principles which was accepted and approved equally by a Committee of the American Bar Association and a Committee of Publishers and Associations.

In no way is it legal to reproduce, duplicate, or transmit any part of this document in either electronic means or in printed format. Recording of this publication is strictly prohibited and any storage of this document is not allowed unless with written permission from the publisher. All rights reserved.

The information provided herein is stated to be truthful and consistent, in that any liability, in terms of inattention or otherwise, by any usage or abuse of any policies, processes, or directions contained within is the solitary and utter responsibility of the recipient reader. Under no circumstances will any legal responsibility or blame be held against the publisher for any reparation, damages, or monetary loss due to the information herein, either directly or indirectly.

Respective authors own all copyrights not held by the publisher.

The information herein is offered for informational purposes solely, and is universal as so. The presentation of the information is without contract or any type of guarantee assurance.

The trademarks that are used are without any consent, and the publication of the trademark is without permission or backing by the trademark owner. All trademarks and brands within this book are for clarifying purposes only and are the owned by the owners themselves, not affiliated with this document.

❦ Created with **Vellum**

BOOK DESCRIPTION: ABOUT THIS BOOK

Eating crispy and crunchy fried food is one of the addictions that none of us can ever give up on. And although we are all aware that fried food is packed with unhealthy fats, we find ourselves unable to give up on it because it is tastier than we can imagine. But have you ever imagined that you can stop depriving yourselves from the delicious taste of fried food? To help you achieve this objective; we have thought of a smarter decision to help you enjoy fried food that will not harm your health anymore. And the core of this healthy frying method is the revolutionary cooking appliance; Air Fryer. Indeed, using an air fryer has become one of the healthiest frying methods that we have ever tried. With the help of air fryer, say good bye to eating restrictions because this book will provide you with succulent recipes. There is no need to worry about saturated fats, because this book will allow you to enjoy guilt free and completely healthy recipes. So if you are willing to enjoy an incredibly tasty variety of dishes without using a high quantity of oil; then this book is the perfect choice for you. This incredible simple Air Fryer Cook Book will let you enjoy the taste of crunchy onion rings, toasts and French Fries as well as a wide range of other choices. What are you waiting for; race to get the best air fried taste in our Vegan and healthy recipe book.

INTRODUCTION

I WANT to thank you and congratulate you for downloading the book, titled "RACE TO TASTE THE HEALTHIEST AIR FRIED RECIPES". For many long years, we have learned so many facts about the harmful effects of fried food; especially with the huge quantity of oil we use and we thought the best solution is to keep away from the fried food and opt for a healthier lifestyle. Indeed, following a conventional diet based on eating junk food and deep fried dishes will lead to detrimental and harmful effects on our health. It is indeed believed that deep fried food can be a primary cause of cardiovascular diseases and high levels of cholesterol. So why would you destroy your health with fatty ingredients? How about a completely new and innovative way that allows you to eat crispy food? Because we care so much about your health, we have looked for a new method to help you enjoy the crispy taste of fried food until we finally managed to discover the revolutionary cooking appliance; Air Fryer. With our Air Fryer; you will be able to fry your food without submerging it into a huge quantity of oil. And you're your food won't be in contact with oil anymore. All that you need to fry your food in Air Fryer is one or two tablespoons of oil. But what is an air fryer and how does it work that it doesn't need so much oil? An air Fryer is, by definition; a cooking device that is made of a closed room or chamber where the hot air is introduced to it with the help of a fan. Inside the air fryer, we find an inner chamber that is programmed to keep stirring the food until it is perfectly fried and by following this cooking method. Food, within air fryers, gets lightly covered by oil and thereby gets fried easily without absorbing oil. And what is most fascinating about air fryer is that you don't have to worry about burning your food because the temperature in the majority of the air fryers doesn't exceed 390° F, but you will have the same crunchy taste and the crispiness you want. We can say that the use of Air Fryer has saved us from the dilemma of harmful fats with just one tablespoon of oil. And to keep the momentum going, we are going to offer you a wide range of food that you never thought you could cook in air fryer. The mouth watering taste of our recipes will leave you unable to decide which recipe to make from Spring rolls, to soufflés and, French fries. And because of its multiuse, there is no doubt that Air Fryers have become very popular during the year 2015. You will see that with our Air fryer, you will be able to bake, fry, steam and also grill a plethora of recipes in a convenient and easy as well as fast way. Let us get ready to start "THE RACE FOR THE BEST AIR FRIED FOOD TASTE" with this book. We hope that you enjoy using the book and the Air fryer alike; just like all the people around the glove. You will find recipes from all the continents and from different culinary traditions. And what is most special about this air fryer book is that you are going to learn extremely healthy as well as balanced-Vegan recipes that will inspire you and satisfy your friends and your family.

GENERAL TIPS FOR THE FIRST AIR FRYER USE

1. Always preheat your air fryer for about 3 minutes before

using it to your desired temperature
2. When you make small bites like croquettes and wings; make sure to shake the basket twice during the cooking process. In this way, you will help cooking the food inside evenly.
3. Do never overcrowd your cooking basket because it will impact the circulation of hot air within the food and hence it will affect the crispiness of the obtained food.
4. Using spray is an excellent oil choice to air fry food. You can also use it to oil the bottom of your air fryer, so that it won't stick.
5. Preheat the Air fryer for 3 minutes. This is sufficient time for the Air fryer to reach the desired temperature.
6. Remove any excess of fat in case you are cooking high-fats ingredients like chicken wings.
7. When you want to fry marinated ingredients; make sure to pat it dry with a clean paper towel before putting it in the basket of your air fryer.
8. When you use a parchment paper or a foil, try to trim it and leave about ½ inch of space around the bottom edge of the air fryer basket.

CHAPTER ONE

AIR FRYER BREAKFAST RECIPES

RECIPE 1: Blueberry oats Breakfast casserole
(Cooking Time: 50 minutes\ Preparation Time: 90 minutes\ Servings: 7)

- **NOTE:**

What is better than starting your day with a healthy breakfast made of nutty oats with the taste of cinnamon? You will like the crispy taste of the oatmeal cookie and the crumbly fruits. If you make this healthy recipe; you will never forget its flavour and it will provide you with the energy you need for a great start of day.

INGREDIENTS:

- 2 Tablespoons of ground flaxseed
- 6 Tablespoons of warm water
- 2 Cups of whole rolled oats
- ½ Cup of slivered almonds
- ½ Cup of hemp seeds
- ⅔ Cup of coconut flakes
- ¼ Cup of coconut sugar

- 1 Teaspoon of baking powder
- 1 Teaspoon of cinnamon
- ¾ Teaspoon of sea salt
- ¾ Cup of Unsweetened Vanilla at the room temperature
- ¼ Cup of maple syrup
- 3 Tablespoons of melted coconut oil
- 1 Chopped banana
- 1 Cup of sliced strawberries
- ½ Cup blueberries

Directions:

1. Preheat your air fryer to about 350° F and grease a baking tray that fits your steamer basket
2. Mix the flaxseed and the warm water into a medium bowl and set the mixture aside for about 5 minutes; don't forget to reserve about 2 tablespoons of hemp seeds, coconut flakes and almonds.
3. In a large, bowl; mix the remaining quantity of hemp seeds; coconut flakes and almonds
4. Add the cinnamon, the baking powder, the salt and brown sugar.
5. In a large bowl, mix altogether the maple syrup, the almond milk, and the coconut oil; then whisk your ingredients very well until it becomes smooth.
6. Add in the mixture of the flaxseed and blend it very well until it becomes smooth.
7. Pour your wet ingredients into your dry ingredients in a medium bowl; then whisk again
8. Layer the strawberries and the bananas into your already prepared baking tray; then spread the mixture of the oats right on the surface

9. Top with the almonds, the blueberries; the coconut flakes and the hemp seeds
10. Cover your tray with an aluminum foil paper and put it in the basket of the air fryer; then close the lid and set the timer to about 45 minutes and the temperature to about 345° F
11. When the timer beeps, remove your casserole from the air fryer and set it aside to cool for about 10 minutes
12. Serve and enjoy your nutritious breakfast

NUTRITIONAL INFORMATION

- Calories per serving – 161 calories
- Fat per serving – 3.7 grams
- Total Carbs per serving – 12.2 grams
- Protein per serving – 6.5 grams

CINNAMON ALMOND TOAST

Recipe 2: Cinnamon Almond Toast
(Cooking Time: 5 minutes\ Preparation Time: 15 minutes\ Servings: 3)

- **NOTE:**

If you prefer having a low Carb and delicious, healthy air fried breakfast; then this recipe is the most suitable choice for you. The crispiness of almond with the twist of a sweet glaze makes a succulent and nutritious breakfast. You are going to enjoy this grain-free recipe.

INGREDIENTS

- 6 Slices of Ciabatta bread of ¾ inch of thickness each.
- 1 Cup of Almond Milk
- 1 Tablespoon of maple syrup
- 2 Tablespoons of whole wheat flour
- 1 Tablespoon of nutritional yeast
- 1 Teaspoon of cinnamon
- ¼ Teaspoon of freshly ground nutmeg

- 1 Dash of salt
- A little bit of coconut oil
- For the toppings; use:
- Vegan butter
- Maple syrup
- Fresh fruits

Directions

1. In a medium bowl; mix the almond milk with the flour, the maple syrup and the whole wheat flour
2. Add the nutritional yeast, the cinnamon, the nutmeg and the salt.
3. Put the bread into a greased baking tray and pour your mixture on top of the bread
4. Add the toast of bread above the ingredients
5. Drizzle your ingredients with a little bit of coconut oil and cover the tray with aluminum foil; then close the lid
6. Set the timer to about 5 minutes and the temperature to 345° F
7. When the timer beeps, remove the tray from the air fryer and serve your breakfast with the vegan butter, the maple syrup, and the fresh fruits.

Nutritional information

- Calories per serving – 224.5 calories
- Fat per serving – 17.5 grams
- Total Carbs per serving – 13 grams
- Protein per serving – 7.5 grams

GLUTEN FREE HAM FRITTATA

Recipe 3: Gluten Free Ham Frittata
(Cooking Time: 25 minutes\ Preparation Time: 35 minutes\ Servings: 4)

- **NOTE:**

Have you ever thought that you can enjoy a delicious cheesy breakfast that is not packed with carbohydrates? Wherever you are; you can enjoy this tasty breakfast rich in succulent tastes. And what you will like more about this recipe is that you can prepare it in a tray or in muffin cups. This recipe will make a great joy for you and even for your friend with its wonderful texture.

INGREDIENTS

- To prepare for the crust for your crust use:
- 4 Cups of shredded and peeled shredded celery root
- 4 Tablespoons of melted butter
- 1Teaspoon of kosher salt
- $\frac{1}{4}$ Teaspoon of ground black pepper
- 2 Tablespoon of coconut flour
- 2 Tablespoons of grated Parmesan cheese

- 1 Tablespoon of olive oil
- To prepare the filling:
- Use 6 large eggs
- 1 Cup of light cream
- ¾ Cup of unsweetened almond milk
- ¼ Teaspoon of ground nutmeg
- ½ Teaspoon of kosher salt
- ¼ Teaspoon of ground black pepper
- ½ Cup of frozen thawed and chopped spinach
- 2 Cups of chopped ham
- 1 Cup of sharp shredded cheddar cheese

Directions:

1. Preheat you air fryer to about 390° F; then grease a baking tray that fits your air fryer basket
2. Start by preparing the crust and mix its ingredients very well in a wide bowl
3. Press your mixture into the greased tray; make sure to raise the crust up to the sides and cover the tray with an aluminum foil paper; then close the lid
4. Set the temperature to 390° F and the timer for about 20 minutes; meanwhile, prepare the filling by cracking the eggs and whisking it altogether in a deep and large bowl with the cream, the almond milk, the nutmeg, the salt, and the pepper.
5. When the timer beeps, remove the crust from the air fryer; then add the spinach and a layer of cheese over your baked crust into the bottom of your tray.
6. Pour the mixture of the eggs over the cheese and the ham.
7. Put the tray in the air fryer basket and close the lid
8. Set the temperature to about 350° F and the timer to

about 25 to 30 minutes
9. When the timer beeps, remove the tray from the air fryer and set it aside to cool for about 10 minutes
10. Serve and enjoy!

Nutritional information

- Calories per serving – 308 calories
- Fat per serving – 23 grams
- Total Carbs per serving – 11 grams
- Protein per serving – 16 grams

GRANOLA WITH CHOCOLATE AND HAZELNUTS

Recipe 4: Granola with chocolate and Hazelnuts
(Cooking Time: 15 minutes\ Preparation Time: 30 minutes\ Servings: 9)

- **NOTE:**

You are about to taste a delicious and crispy granola with the succulent taste of hazelnuts and the enjoyable chocolate. You will like this low carb breakfast recipe because of its healthy ingredients.

INGREDIENTS

- 1 and ½ cups of hazelnuts
- 1 and ½ cups of almonds
- 1 Cup of flaxseed meal
- ¼ Cup of cocoa powder
- ½ Teaspoon of salt
- ¼ Cup of melted butter
- ¼ Cup of hazelnut oil
- 2 Oz of unsweetened chocolate
- 1/3 Cup of granulated erythritol

- ½ Teaspoon of hazelnut extract
- 20 drops of stevia extract

Directions

1. Preheat your air fryer to about 300°F and line a baking sheet with a parchment paper.
2. Into a food processor, process the hazelnuts and the almonds until they become crumbly
3. Put the ingredients in a small pot over a medium-low heat and add the flax seed meal, the cocoa powder and the salt.
4. In another small pan and over a low heat, melt the butter; then add the hazelnut oil and the chocolate for about 3 minutes
5. Remove your ingredients from the heat and add the hazelnut and the extract of the stevia extract.
6. Pour the mixture of chocolate over the mixture of nut and toss very well until it is combined.
7. Spread the mixture evenly on the already prepared baking sheet and put it in the basket of the air fryer; then close the lid
8. Set the timer to about 15 minutes and the heat to about 390° F
9. When the timer beeps; remove the ingredients from the air fryer and set aside for 5 minutes
10. Serve and enjoy a crispy breakfast!

Nutritional information

- Calories per serving – 187 calories
- Fat per serving – 17.5 grams

- Total Carbs per serving – 6.3 grams
- Protein per serving – 4.4 grams

AVOCADO EGG BOATS

Recipe 5: Avocado Egg Boats
(Cooking Time: 20 minutes\ Preparation Time: 25 minutes\ Servings: 2)

- **NOTE:**

If you are busy and you don't have so much time to prepare a breakfast, then avocado boats will be your favorite recipe. You will only need a few ingredients and you will eat the tastiest and the healthiest breakfast ever.

INGREDIENTS

- 1 Teaspoon of coconut oil
- 1 Ripe avocado
- 2 Large organic eggs
- 1 Pinch of salt
- 1 Pinch of pepper
- Chopped walnuts
- Pearls, Balsamic
- Use fresh thyme

Directions:

1. Preheat your air fryer to about 385°F and grease a baking tray that fits your air fryer basket with cooking spray
2. Cut your avocado into halves and remove its pit; then scoop out the flesh of the avocado
3. Remove a tiny part of the avocado skin and set it aside
4. In medium bowl; crack your eggs and split it into about 3 small bowls or container
5. Put the egg yolks into glass tea cups and the white yolk into another bowl
6. Add the salt and the pepper
7. Grease a baking tray that fits your air fryer with cooking spray
8. In a shallow, large skillet; sear the avocado halves for about 30 seconds
9. Line the avocados in the baking tray; and fill its cavities with a little bit of egg whites; then evenly divide the egg yolks between the avocado halves and season it with salt and pepper
10. Put the lid of avocados on and put the baking tray in the air fryer; then close the lid
11. Set the temperature to about 350° F and the timer to about 18 minutes
12. When the timer beeps, remove the lid of the air fryer and serve your avocado boats with thyme, walnuts and with the balsamic pearls

Nutritional information

- Calories per serving – 215 calories
- Fat per serving – 18.1 grams

- Total Carbs per serving – 8 grams
- Protein per serving – 9.1 grams

CLOUD PANCAKES WITH SCALLIONS

Recipe 6: Cloud pancakes with scallions

(Cooking Time: 23 minutes\ Preparation Time: 15 minutes\ Servings: 5-6)

- **NOTE:**

These pancake scallion clouds make a great alternative for sandwiches. This recipe is very low in carbohydrates and it is high in proteins and in healthy fat too. Cloud Pancakes are not only delicious by itself, but you can also enjoy it with cucumber salad.

INGREDIENTS:

- 3 Separated Large eggs
- 3 Tablespoons of cream cheese
- 3 Tablespoons of chopped scallions; green onions or you can use chives
- ½ Teaspoon of white or black pepper
- 1 Pinch of sea salt
- 1 Teaspoon of white vinegar

- 2 Tablespoons of coconut oil

Directions:

1. Preheat your air fryer to about 300° F
2. Grease a baking paper with 1 tablespoon of coconut oil and set it aside
3. Separate the eggs and make sure that you don't see yolks in the egg whites
4. Add the whites of eggs to a bowl and put the egg yolks into another bowl
5. Add the scallion, the cream cheese, the pepper and the salt to the egg yolks and set it aside.
6. Add about 1 teaspoon of the white vinegar to the whites of eggs whites and add 1 pinch of salt if needed
7. Whisk the egg whites on a high speed and set it aside
8. Combine the mixture of yolks
9. Pour the mixture of yolks into the whites; but be careful not to over mix.
10. With a wooden spoon, scoop about ¼ cup of mixture and make the shape of rounds on the baking paper (Make the rounds about the size of a cookie or a little bit larger)
11. Using a large spoon or a quarter cup, scoop the mixture into even rounds on the sheet; make sure to leave a small room between the rounds and put the baking sheet in a baking tray
12. Put the baking tray in the air fryer basket and close the lid
13. Set the temperature to about 320° F and the timer to 23 minutes
14. When the timer beeps, remove the baking tray from the air fryer; then serve and enjoy it

Nutritional information

- Calories per serving – 63 calories
- Fat per serving – 4.75 grams
- Total Carbs per serving – 1.6 grams
- Protein per serving – 3.9 grams

WHOLE WHEAT BURRITOS

Recipe 7: Whole wheat Burritos
(Cooking Time: 5 minutes\ Preparation Time: 20 minutes\ Servings: 1-2)

- **NOTE:**

A healthy and nutritious breakfast that will give you the energy you need to start a busy day. This recipe is perfect for people going a vegan diet; it is low in carb and you won't feel guilty eating it. So how about enjoying your breakfast right now?

INGREDIENTS:

- 2 Cups of Brown Rice
- 1 cup of Vegan Pinto Beans
- 1 Chopped red Onion
- 1 Red Pepper
- Chopped lettuce
- 2 Serrano Peppers
- 1 cup of organic Corn
- 1 Peeled and chopped Avocado

- 1 cup of cheese Sauce
- 1 Cup of diced tomato
- ½ Cup of hot Sauce

Directions:

1. Preheat your air fryer to about 350° F
2. Start by cooking the brown rice in your rice cooker or in a pot.
3. Mix altogether the brown rice and the refried beans.
4. Put the brown rice and the bean mixture right into the middle of the tortilla and add the rest of your ingredients right on top
5. Wrap your burrito and put it over an aluminum foil paper
6. Lay the aluminum foil in the basket of the air fryer with the burrito inside; then close the lid and set the timer to about 5 minutes and the temperature to about 345° F
7. When the timer beeps, remove the burrito from the air fryer; then serve and enjoy it!

Nutritional information

- Calories per serving – 242.3 calories
- Fat per serving – 18 grams
- Total Carbs per serving – 13.2 grams
- Protein per serving – 16.7 grams

Recipe 8: Air Fried Quiche muffins
(Cooking Time: 25 minutes\ Preparation Time: 10 minutes\ Servings: 12)

- **NOTE:**

This is a healthy and very easy breakfast recipe and its taste will stick to your mind for eternity. You can make this quiche recipe in only a few minutes while you are getting ready to go to your work.

INGREDIENTS

To make the base, use:

- 12 large eggs
- ½ Cup of heavy cream
- ¼ Cup of milk
- 2 Tablespoons of fresh chopped parsley
- 2 Tablespoons of fresh chopped basil
- ¼ Teaspoon of salt
- ¼ Teaspoon of pepper
- 1 Cup of broccoli; broken into florets
- 1 Cup of freshly cut spinach
- 1 Finely chopped red bell pepper
- ½ Cup of finely diced onion
- 1 Seeded and finely diced jalapeno pepper
- ½ Cup of cheddar cheese
- 1 Pound of finely cut chicken

Directions:

1. Cook the chicken and cut it into small cubes.
2. Preheat your air fryer to about 375° F
3. Grease a non-stick muffin tin with coconut oil and in a large bowl mix the cream with the eggs, the parsley, the basil, the salt, and the pepper; then set the mixture aide and wash all of your veggies
4. Cut the veggies into small cubes and toss it into the bowl in which you have put your veggies
5. Add half the quantity of the cheese and the chicken meat

6. Put around ¼ cup of the mixture and pour it in the muffin tin; then repeat the same process with the rest of the muffins and top with cheese on top of each
7. Put the muffin pan in the basket of your air fryer and close the lid
8. Set the timer to about 25 minutes and the temperature to 365° F
9. When the timer beeps, remove the muffin pan from the air fryer and set it aside to cool for about 10 minutes
10. Serve and enjoy your quiche

Nutritional information

- Calories per serving – 166 calories
- Fat per serving – 7.3 grams
- Total Carbs per serving – 9.2 grams
- Protein per serving – 17 grams

AIR FRIED PANCAKES

Recipe 9: Air Fried pancakes

(Cooking Time: 5 minutes\ Preparation Time: 3 minutes\ Servings: 6-7)

- **NOTE:**

Have you ever wanted to enjoy eating pancakes without having to worry about how much carbohydrates it has? With this recipe; it is time to enjoy this delicious pancake taste because it will help you lose weight with its low carb count.

INGREDIENTS

- ½ Tablespoon of butter
- 2 Large eggs
- 2.5 Oz of cream cheese

Directions:

1. In a medium bowl, mix the cream cheese with the eggs and keep whisking until it becomes fluffy and creamy

2. Let the batter aside for about 4 minutes
3. Grease the air fryer baking tray with cooking spray and pour in 1 tea cup of the pancake batter
4. Put the baking tray in the basket of your air fryer; then close the lid
5. Set the temperature to about 365° F and the timer to about 5 minutes
6. When the timer beeps, remove the pancake from the air fryer
7. Repeat the same process to make the number of pancake until your run out of butter
8. Serve and enjoy your pancakes!

Nutritional information

- Calories per serving – 388 calories
- Fat per serving – 34.9 grams
- Total Carbs per serving – 2.6 grams
- Protein per serving – 16.7 grams

AIR FRIED PANCAKES

Recipe 10: Air Fried pancakes

(Cooking Time: 4 minutes\ Preparation Time: 2 minutes\ Servings: 2)

- NOTE:

What is better than the combination of butter and eggs? Having scrambled eggs with butter makes a perfect breakfast to start your day with; it is a very easy recipe to make in a just four minute.

INGREDIENTS:

- 2 Teaspoons of butter
- 4 Eggs
- 2 Tablespoons of low fat milk
- ¼ Teaspoon of baking powder
- ½ Teaspoon of salt1 Pinch of black pepper
- ½ Cup of grated low-fat cheddar cheese

Directions:

1. Crack the eggs in a medium bowl, and whisk it with the milk, the baking powder, the salt and the black pepper

until it becomes perfectly combined; then set it aside for about 5 minutes
2. Grease a small non-stick baking pan that fits your air fryer with cooking spray: then pour in 1 tablespoon of butter
3. Whisk your eggs and add to it the cheese; then pour it into the greased baking tray
4. Put the tray in the basket of the air fryer and close the lid
5. Set the timer to about 4 to 5 minutes and the heat to about 325° F
6. When the timer beeps, remove the baking tray from the air fryer; then serve and enjoy your scrambled eggs

Nutritional information

- Calories per serving – 186.6 calories
- Fat per serving – 13.8 grams
- Total Carbs per serving – 1.5 grams
- Protein per serving – 13.1 grams

CHAPTER TWO

LUNCH RECIPES

- **Chicken Recipes**

RECIPE 11: Chicken with garlic and olives

(Cooking Time: 15 minutes\ Preparation Time: 7 minutes\ Servings: 3-4)

- **NOTE:**

Are you still thinking what you can cook for lunch? If yes, then this recipe is absolutely the one for you; it is low in Carbs; easy-to make and mouthwatering. No one will be able to resist the delicious taste of crumbly feta with the chicken breasts; a heavenly taste you will get addicted to.

INGREDIENTS:

- 4 large skinless and boneless chicken breasts
- 1 Tablespoon of olive oil
- ½ Teaspoon of salt
- ½ Teaspoon of ground black pepper
- 1 Can of diced tomatoes
- 1 Teaspoon of garlic powder
- ½ Cup of crumbled Feta Cheese
- ½ Cup of large sliced green olive

Directions

1. Start by preheating your air fryer to about 390° F
2. Trim any excess of fat and any small undesirable parts from the chicken
3. Make crosswise small slits in each of the breasts
4. Rub your chicken breasts with 1 pinch of salt and 1 pinch of black pepper; then add the ground rosemary
5. Grease a baking tray with cooking spray and arrange the chicken breasts in it
6. Drizzle the chicken with more olive oil and put the tray in the basket of the air fryer; then close the lid
7. Set the timer to about 10 minutes and the temperature to about 350° F; shake the air fryer basket once or twice
8. While the chicken is being cooked; mix the tomatoes with the garlic powder; a little bit of salt and ground pepper
9. Finely slice the olives and crumble the Feta
10. When the timer of the air fryer beeps; remove the chicken from the air fryer; then spoon you tomato mixture around your chicken pieces
11. Put the chicken back in the air fryer; then close the lid and set the timer to about 3 to 4 minutes and set the temperature to about 350° F
12. When the timer beeps, remove the chicken from the air fryer and top with the Feta and the green olives and put it back for about 5 additional minutes
13. Serve and enjoy!

Nutritional information

- Calories per serving – 284.9 calories
- Fat per serving – 12.2 grams

- Total Carbs per serving - 10.7 grams
- Protein per serving - 32 grams

CRISPY CHICKEN LIVERS

Recipe 12: Crispy Chicken Livers

(Cooking Time: 15 minutes\ Preparation Time: 5 minutes\ Servings: 4)

- **NOTE:**

Chicken liver is one of the cheapest and the most delicious protein ingredients ever. The twist of chicken liver with pepper with makes your dish extraordinary. Besides; air frying chicken won't take so much time; you will get your meal ready in a blink of an eye.

INGREDIENTS:

- 1 Pound of chicken liver
- 1 Large, finely chopped onion
- 5 Minced garlic cloves
- 1 Inch of finely chopped ginger
- 7 Chopped small chilies
- 1 Finely chopped, small bunch of cilantro
- 1 sprig of curry leaves
- ½ Teaspoon of Garam Masala
- 1 Teaspoon of Chili powder

- ¼ Teaspoon of pepper powder
- ½ Teaspoon of turmeric powder
- 1 Tablespoon of oil
- 1 pinch of salt

Directions:

1. Start by cleaning the chicken liver and remove any excess of fats and wash it with tap water
2. Pat the chicken liver dry with clean towels or with paper towels; then grease a baking tray that fits the air fryer with cooking spray
3. Put the chicken liver in the greased tray and add the onions; the curry leaves and the ginger
4. Add the garlic, the chilies, the chili powder and the turmeric and whisk very well.
5. Toss in the chicken liver and stir very well; then season with salt, the pepper powder and the chopped cilantro
6. Drizzle with a little bit more of oil and put the tray in the air fryer basket; then close the lid
7. Set the temperature to about 385° F and the timer to about 15 minutes
8. When the timer beeps, remove the tray from the air fryer and serve the chicken liver hot
9. Garnish with the chopped cilantro and top with the Garam Masala
10. Enjoy a taste you will never forget!

Nutritional information

- Calories per serving – 253 calories
- Fat per serving – 10.2 grams
- Total Carbs per serving –7.2 grams
- Protein per serving – 31.2 grams

CHICKEN WITH BROCCOLI AND SESAME

Recipe 13: Chicken with broccoli and sesame
(Cooking Time: 20 minutes\ Preparation Time: 35 minutes\ Servings: 5)

- **NOTE:**

Sesame and chicken make a delicious staple that is worth of taking out with you even in picnics. With the crispy and the salty, sweet twist, you are going to feel that you have travelled into a world of dreams. This recipe makes a classic and tasty dish; you will not only like it; but you will lick your fingers after eating it.

INGREDIENTS:

- 4 Boneless and skinless chicken breasts
- 2 and ½ tablespoons of tapioca flour
- 2 Cups of broccoli florets
- 1 Medium head of cauliflower
- 1 Tablespoon of sesame seeds
- 3 Tablespoons of tamari
- 1 Tablespoon of sesame oil
- 1 Tablespoon of sriracha

- ¼ Teaspoon of red pepper flakes
- 1 Tablespoon of oyster sauce
- 1 Teaspoon of maple syrup
- 2 Tablespoons of chicken broth
- 2 Tablespoon of coconut oil
- 1 Pinch of salt
- 1 Pinch of pepper
- 1 Finely chopped garlic clove
- 1 Teaspoon of chopped ginger
- 1 Tablespoon of sliced green onions

Directions

1. Wash the chicken breasts and pat it dry with paper towels; then season it with a little bit of salt and 1 pinch of pepper
2. Cut the chicken into cubes and coat it with the tapioca flour; then set it aside for about 10 minutes
3. Now, prepare the cauliflower rice by cutting the cauliflower head into little florets and discarding its core
4. Chop the rice into very small parts and process it with a food processor
5. Boil 1 and ½ cups of water in a medium saucepan and steam the broccoli rice in it for about 5 minutes on a medium- high heat; then drain it in a colander and set it aside
6. Preheat the air fryer to about 375° F
7. Grease a baking tray that fits your air fryer and put the chicken it; then toss in the garlic and the ginger with the chicken
8. Add the tamari, the sriracha and mix very well; then add the sesame seeds, the red pepper flakes and the

maple syrup
9. Add the broccoli rice and drizzle with coconut oil and top with green onion slices
10. Pour in the 2 tablespoons of broth and put the tray in the basket of the air fryer
11. Close the lid of the air fryer and set the timer to about 20 minutes and the heat to about 350° F
12. When the timer beeps, remove the baking tray from the air fryer; then set it aside to cool for 5 minutes
13. Serve and enjoy your delicious lunch!

Nutritional information

- Calories per serving – 427 calories
- Fat per serving – 28.6 grams
- Total Carbs per serving –12.5 grams
- Protein per serving – 46 grams

CHICKEN WITH SESAME AND ORANGE SAUCE

Recipe 14: Chicken with sesame and Orange sauce

(Cooking Time: 20 minutes\ Preparation Time: 10 minutes\ Servings: 5)

- **NOTE:**

You may find it strange to have chicken with orange sauce; but once you taste it, you will realize that the flavor is just stunning. This recipe is creative and delicious; it is perfect to make in special occasions.

INGREDIENTS:

- 2 Pounds of skinless and boneless chicken thighs
- 1 Tablespoon of cornstarch
- ¼ Cup of coconut flour
- 1 Pinch of salt
- 1 Pinch of pepper
- 3 Tablespoons of coconut oil
- To prepare the sauce:
- 1 Tablespoon of chopped ginger
- ¼ Cup of orange juice
- 2 Tablespoons of fish sauce

- 2 Tablespoons of soy sauce
- 1 and ½ teaspoons of orange extract
- 2 Teaspoons of sweetener
- 1 Cup of maple syrup
- ½ Teaspoon of ground coriander
- 1 Tablespoon of orange zest
- ¼ Teaspoon of red pepper flakes
- ¼ Teaspoon of sesame seeds
- 2 Tablespoons of chopped scallions

Directions:

1. Start by chopping the chicken meat into small sized pieces and mix the cornstarch with the coconut flour into a deep bowl; then season it with 1 pinch of pepper and 1 pinch of salt
2. Add the chicken meat to the mixture of the flour and toss your mixture very well
3. Preheat your air fryer to about 390° F and grease a baking pan with cooking spray
4. Put the chicken into your greased tray and put it in the air fryer; then close the lid
5. Set the timer to 9 minutes and the temperature to about 375° F
6. When the timer beeps, remove the chicken from the air fryer. In the mean time, mix the orange juice with the fish sauce, the soy sauce, the orange extract, the sweetener, the water, and the coriander into a food processor and process it until it becomes smooth
7. Pour the obtained extract into a medium saucepan and let is simmer on a medium fire for about 3 minutes
8. Add the chicken with the sesame seeds, the orange zest, the red pepper flakes and the scallions and cook

  for 1 additional minute
9. Remove the orange sauce from the heat and serve your chicken into serving dishes
10. Enjoy a delicious lunch!

Nutritional information

- Calories per serving – 422 calories
- Fat per serving – 20 grams
- Total Carbs per serving –6.1 grams
- Protein per serving – 45 grams

CHICKEN WITH PARMESAN CHEESE

Recipe 15: Chicken with Parmesan cheese

(Cooking Time: 25 minutes\ Preparation Time: 5 minutes\ Servings: 4)

- **NOTE:**

This chicken recipe is one of the healthiest recipes you can ever taste because it can be eaten with any diet. And while there is no use of breadcrumbs in this lunch, you won't even notice it because you will enjoy the taste of the pasta sauce with the melting cheese under your teeth. Chicken with Parmesan cheese is just what you need to feel satisfied.

INGREDIENTS:

- 2 Skinless and boneless chicken breasts
- ½ Cup of sugar-free spaghetti sauce
- ½ Cup of shredded mozzarella cheese
- 1 Teaspoon of grated parmesan cheese
- 1 Pinch of garlic salt
- ½ teaspoon of Italian seasoning

Directions

1. Preheat your air fryer to about 375° F
2. Grease a baking tray with cooking spray
3. Season the chicken meat with a little bit of garlic salt and with the Italian seasoning
4. Put the chicken breasts in the greased baking tray
5. Pour in the pasta sauce on top of your chicken breasts
6. Put the baking tray in the basket of the air fryer and close the lid
7. Set the temperature to about 370° F and the timer to 25 minutes
8. When the timer beeps remove the tray from the air fryer; top with cheese; then serve and enjoy your lunch!

Nutritional information

- Calories per serving – 216.8calories
- Fat per serving –9.3 grams
- Total Carbs per serving –0.8 grams
- Protein per serving – 30.5 grams

TURKEY BREAST WITH THYME AND SAGE

Recipe 16: Turkey breast with thyme and sage
(Cooking Time: 25 minutes\ Preparation Time: 15 minutes\ Servings: 5-6)

- **NOTE:**

Have you ever tried roasting turkey breasts in an air fryer? If you haven't tried it yet, you have missed a lot because the taste of the air fried turkey meat is irresistible; it is incredibly succulent that you will be able to eat the meat by yourself. You can serve this recipe with salad and lemon wedges.

INGREDIENTS:

- 2 Teaspoons of coconut oil
- 4 Pounds of whole turkey breasts
- 1 Teaspoon of dried thyme
- ½ Teaspoon of dried sage
- ½ Teaspoon of smoked paprika
- 1 Teaspoon of salt
- ½ Teaspoon of freshly ground black pepper
- ¼ Cup of maple syrup
- 2 Tablespoons of Dijon mustard

- 1 Tablespoon of butter

Directions:

1. Start by preheating your air fryer to about 350°F.
2. Rub the turkey breast with the oil and in a small bowl, mix the thyme, the sage, the paprika, the salt and the pepper; then rub your turkey breast with the mixture of the spices.
3. Transfer your seasoned breast to your air fryer basket and close the lid
4. Set the timer to about 25 minutes and the temperature to about 350° F
5. When the timer beeps, flip the turkey breast on the other side and cook it for 10 additional minutes. In the mean time, prepare the glaze by combining altogether the mustard and the maple syrup in a small saucepan; then add the butter and put the saucepan on a medium heat for about 3 minutes
6. When the timer beeps, remove the breast from the air fryer and brush it with the glaze.
7. Set the turkey breast aside to cool and cover it with a foil tin; then set it aside for about 10 minutes before slicing and serving the turkey meat
8. Enjoy!

Nutritional information

- Calories per serving – 161.1 calories
- Fat per serving –6.3 grams
- Total Carbs per serving –0.0 grams
- Protein per serving – 24.3 grams

CHICKEN PIZZA

Recipe 17: Chicken Pizza

(Cooking Time: 20 minutes\ Preparation Time: 10 minutes\ Servings: 4-5)

- **NOTE:**

Are you looking for an exciting way to cook your pizza? This recipe will provide you with low carb ingredients that will satisfy you. This chicken pizza is very high in protein and will make a great choice for your diet.

INGREDIENTS

- 1 and ½ cups of part skim shredded mozzarella cheese
- 2 Teaspoons of salted butter
- ¾ Cup of Baking Mix
- 2 Teaspoons of Italian seasoning
- 1 Teaspoon of baking powder
- ½ Teaspoon of garlic salt
- ½ Teaspoon of yeast
- 2 Large eggs

- 2 Tablespoons of water

For the toppings:

- 1 Cup of pizza sauce
- 1 Cup of shredded mozzarella cheese
- 1 Pound of shredded chicken meat
- 1 Thinly sliced onion
- 1 Cut green pepper
- 1 and ½ cups of sliced
- Slices of pepperoni

Directions:

1. Melt the mozzarella cheese in a small pan over a medium heat with the butter for about 3 minutes; make sure to stir; meanwhile, mix your dry ingredients with the eggs and the water
2. Knead the obtained dough for about 4 minutes with your hands; then lay the dough into a plastic wrap and set it aside for about 15 minutes
3. Preheat your air fryer to 350° F and grease a pizza baking tray with cooking spray; then spread the pizza dough in it and put it in the basket of the air fryer
4. Close the lid and set the timer to about 5 minutes and the temperature to about 375° F
5. When the timer beeps, remove the pizza crust from the air fryer and top it with the sauce, the mozzarella cheese, the ground cooked and shredded chicken meat and the pepperoni
6. Put the pizza again in the basket of the air fryer and close the lid
7. Set the timer to about 5 minutes and the heat to 350° F
8. When the timer beeps, remove the pizza from the air

fryer; then serve and enjoy it with olive and other veggies.

Nutritional information

- Calories per serving – 180.2 calories
- Fat per serving –11 grams
- Total Carbs per serving –1.8 grams
- Protein per serving – 17.3 grams

ALMOND CRUSTED CHICKEN

Recipe 18: Almond Crusted Chicken

(Cooking Time: 12 minutes\ Preparation Time: 5 minutes\ Servings: 4)

- **NOTE:**

This recipe is special because you the breading can be substituted with the use of chopped almonds. It is a very healthy and low carb recipe with a twist of calcium; it is delicious; it is fast and easy-to-make.

INGREDIENTS:

- ½ Cup of salted almonds
- ¼ Cup of seasoned breadcrumbs
- 4 Chicken breasts or 1 pound of boneless and skinless chicken meat
- ¼ Cup of Dijon mustard
- 2 Tablespoons of oil
- 1 Tablespoon of butter
- 1 Cup of parmesan cheese
- 1 Pinch of salt
- Lemon wedges

Directions:

1. Put the almonds and the breadcrumbs altogether into a food processor and pulse it until it becomes crumbly
2. Put the crumbly mixture over a plate
3. Preheat your air fryer to 365° F
4. Grease a baking tray with a cooking spray and put the chicken in the basket of the air fryer
5. Close the lid of the air fryer and set the timer to about 12 minutes and the temperature to about 375° F
6. When the timer beeps, remove the chicken meat from the air fryer; then serve and enjoy it with lemon wedges and parmesan

Nutritional information

- Calories per serving – 323 calories
- Fat per serving –19 grams
- Total Carbs per serving –9.5 grams
- Protein per serving – 29.1 grams

PISTACHIO STUFFED CHICKEN

Recipe 19: Pistachio stuffed chicken

(Cooking Time: 25 minutes\ Preparation Time: 8 minutes\ Servings: 6)

- **NOTE:**

This recipe will teach you how to cook chicken in an innovative new method. It is a gluten-free chicken recipe that you will enjoy and it is very elegant that you can serve it in special occasion. Chicken stuffed with pistachios is one of the most very well balanced meals you have ever tasted.

INGREDIENTS:

- 1 Cup of shelled unsalted pistachios
- 1 Minced garlic clove
- ½ Tablespoon of grainy Dijon mustard
- ¼ Cup of lemon juice
- 2 Pounds of flattened chicken breast
- 2 Tablespoons of olive oil

Directions:

1. Preheat your air fryer to about 390° F and grease a

baking tray with a cooking spray and set it aside.
2. Pulse your pistachios, the garlic, the mustard and about ¼ cup of lemon juice and combine it very well
3. Spread the pistachio mustard of one of the sides of your flattened chicken breast and then roll it up.
4. Rub the rolled chicken breasts with a little bit of olive oil; then sprinkle with a little bit of salt and 1 pinch of pepper
5. Drizzle the chicken meat with more lemon juice and drizzle with more lemon juice
6. Cover the chicken meat with aluminum foil tin and put it in the greased baking tray
7. Close the lid of the air fryer and set the timer for about 20 minutes and the temperature for about 375° F
8. When the timer beeps, remove the chicken from the air fryer and set it aside to cool for about 5 minutes
9. Serve and enjoy your pistachio stuffed chicken

Nutritional information

- Calories per serving – 227 calories
- Fat per serving –17 grams
- Total Carbs per serving –9.8 grams
- Protein per serving – 8.3 grams

CHICKEN BALLS WITH TOMATO SAUCE

Recipe 20: Chicken balls with tomato sauce
(Cooking Time: 25 minutes\ Preparation Time: 15 minutes\ Servings: 4)

- NOTE:

This recipe is one of the favorite recipes for most of the people; it is spiced with a delicious sweet taste. This recipe is simple; easy and creative; you are going to enjoy it!

INGREDIENTS:

- ½ Pound of minced chicken
- 1 Cup of roughly chopped onions
- 1 Large egg
- 2 Tablespoons of raisins
- 1 Tablespoon of chopped parsley
- ½ Tablespoon of ground black pepper
- ½ Cup of breadcrumbs
- ½ Teaspoon of salt
- For the sauce: ½ cup of hot sauce+ 1 cup of brown

sugar+2 tablespoons of apple cider vinegar+ 1 pinch of salt

Directions:

1. Put all of your ingredients into a large and deep bowl.
2. Combine all of your ingredients very well and make the shape of balls from the chicken meat
3. Put the chicken balls in a greased baking tray and put it in the basket of your air fryer
4. Close the lid of the air fryer and set the timer to about 18 minutes and the temperature for about 365° F; meanwhile, prepare the sauce by mixing ½ cup of hot sauce with 1 cup of light brown sugar and 2 tablespoons of apple cider vinegar; sprinkle with salt and cook for about 5 minutes on a low heat.
5. When the timer beeps, remove the chicken balls from the air fryer and serve it with tomato sauce. Enjoy!

Nutritional information

- Calories per serving – 150 calories
- Fat per serving –9.1 grams
- Total Carbs per serving –9 grams
- Protein per serving – 2.3 grams
- **Beef and Pork Lunch Recipes**

Recipe 21: Beef curry
(Cooking Time: 30 minutes\ Preparation Time: 15 minutes\ Servings: 3-4)

- **NOTE:**

This beef curry recipe is very healthy cooked and rich in fiber as well as spices. It is one of the favorite main dishes for most of the people around the globe; you are going to enjoy every bite.

INGREDIENTS:

- 2 Pounds of cubed Beef meat
- 2 Tablespoons of Coriander powder
- 2 Tablespoons of turmeric powder
- 1 Tablespoons of ginger garlic paste
- 2 Tablespoons of chili powder
- 2 Tablespoons of pepper powder
- 1 Tablespoon of Garam Masala powder
- 1 Teaspoon of fennel seed powder
- 2 Finely sliced green or white onions
- 1 Finely cubed tomato
- 2 Tablespoons of olive oil
- 1 Pinch of salt
- Leaves of curry

Directions:

1. Preheat your air fryer to about 390° F
2. Clean the cubed beef and season it with about 2 tablespoons of coriander powder; 1 teaspoon of turmeric powder, 2 tablespoons of ginger garlic paste, 2 tablespoons of chili powder, 1 tablespoon of pepper powder, 1 teaspoon of Garam Masala powder, 1 teaspoon of fennel seed powder and 1 pinch of salt.
3. Cook the beef meat in boiling water over a medium high heat for about 15 minutes
4. Drain the beef meat and pat it dry with a paper towel
5. Grease a baking tray and put the beef meat in it; adjust the seasoning of salt and pepper

6. Drizzle with oil; then put the tray in the basket of the air fryer and close the lid
7. Set the timer to about 15 minutes and the temperature to 350°; in the meantime; put a medium saucepan over a medium heat and pour in 2 tablespoons of oil
8. Add the onion and sauté it for 3 minutes; then add to it the turmeric powder, the coriander powder and the pepper
9. Add the tomato and cook it very well and pour in ½ cup of water; then let simmer for 10 minutes
10. Add the curry leaves and the salt
11. When the timer beeps, remove the beef meat from the air fryer and serve it with the sauce and rice

Nutritional information

- Calories per serving −268.2 calories
- Fat per serving −8.1 grams
- Total Carbs per serving −11.3 grams
- Protein per serving − 37.2 grams

BEEF ROULADEN

Recipe 22: Beef Rouladen

(Cooking Time: 40 minutes\ Preparation Time: 20 minutes\ Servings: 3-4)

- **NOTE:**

Beef Rouladen is one of the German favorite traditional recipes. Beef roulade has unique taste with the gravy and the nutmeg. You can make this recipe anytime of the day; it is perfect for dinners and special occasions.

INGREDIENTS

- 4 Oz of fresh bread crumbs
- 2 Oz of sugar-free chopped bacon
- ½ Cup of chopped parsley
- 2 Teaspoon of dried marjoram
- ½ Teaspoon of peeled and grated lemon
- 2 Large eggs
- 1 Pinch of nutmeg
- 1 Pinch of salt
- 1 Pinch of pepper
- 1 Cup of water or vegetable stock

- 2 Pounds of top sirloin or of bottom round
- 1 Finely diced onion
- 1 Cup of chopped mushrooms
- 4 Tablespoons of butter
- 2 Cups of beef stock
- 1 Tablespoon of coconut flour combined with a little bit of water

Directions:

1. Mix the bread crumbs, the bacon; the parsley, the marjoram, the lemon peel, the eggs, the nutmeg or the allspice and the salt; then sprinkle with a little bit of pepper.
2. Moisten your ingredients with vegetable stock or water until the ingredients start holding on together; then set it aside
3. While the beef is being marinated; put the onion in a large wok and sauté it with 1 tablespoon of butter
4. Add the mushrooms and sauté for about 5 minutes
5. Preheat your air fryer to about 375° F
6. To prepare the beef, cut the beef meat into slices of 3/8 inch f thickness each
7. Now, pound the slices of beef meat gently until you form squares of meat
8. Season with the salt and the pepper; then sprinkle with about 1 tablespoons of the mixture of the bread crumbs into each of the squares of beef
9. Roll the beef meat towards its end until you finish the meat
10. Line the beef meat in a greased baking tray and drizzle with a little bit of oil
11. Put the baking tray in the basket of the air fryer and

close the lid
12. Set the timer to 25 minutes and the temperature to about 325° F
13. When the timer beeps, remove the beef meat from the air fryer and prepare the slurry with the coconut flour and the 1 cup of tomato sauce
14. Let the sauce boil, and season it with pepper, salt and a little bit of oil; then let simmer for about 3 minutes
15. Remove the sauce from the saucepan and serve the slices of meat with the sauce
16. Enjoy!

Nutritional information

- Calories per serving –243.5 calories
- Fat per serving –9 grams
- Total Carbs per serving –5.2 grams
- Protein per serving – 29.6 grams

BEEF MEAT JERKY

Recipe 23: Beef meat Jerky

(Cooking Time: 6 minutes\ Preparation Time: 5 minutes\ Servings: 2-3)

- **NOTE:**

Beef jerky is one of the healthiest low-carb recipes that you can ever make. Beef jerky is not only nutritious, but it is delicious too and very easy-to make

INGREDIENTS:

- 2 Mignons of filets
- 2 Teaspoons of coarse salt
- 1 and ½ teaspoons of freshly ground black pepper
- 1 Teaspoon of olive oil
- 1/8 teaspoon of cayenne pepper
- 2 Oz of crumbled blue cheese
- 1 Tablespoon of divided butter
- 1 and ½ teaspoons of cannabis infused butter
- 2 Teaspoons of finely chopped fresh chives

Directions:

1. Season the steaks of beef on the two sides with a little bit of salt and 1 pinch of ground pepper
2. Preheat your air fryer to about 375° F
3. Grease a baking tray with cooking spray; then add the steaks and drizzle it with a little bit of coconut oil
4. Add the butter and put the baking tray in the basket of the air fryer; then close the lid
5. Set the timer to 6 minutes and the temperature to about 350°F
6. When the timer beeps, remove the steaks from the air fryer and pour the melted butter on top of the steaks; then sprinkle with cheese
7. Serve and enjoy!

Nutritional information

- Calories per serving –210 calories
- Fat per serving –8 grams
- Total Carbs per serving –7.9 grams
- Protein per serving – 25 grams

Recipe 24: Beef Casserole with Cheese
(Cooking Time: 20 minutes\ Preparation Time: 10 minutes\ Servings: 4)

- **NOTE:**

In your quest to enjoy healthy food; this recipe will be the best so far. This cheesy beef casserole is rich in proteins and in nutrients; you are going to enjoy its delicious and healthy taste.
INGREDIENTS:

- 1 and ½ pounds of ground beef

- ½ Can of minced tomatoes
- 2 Oz of pickled jalapeños
- 7 Oz of shredded Monterey Jack
- 1 Cup of sour cream
- 1 Finely chopped scallion
- 2 Tablespoons of butter
- 2 Teaspoons of chili powder
- 2 Teaspoons of paprika powder
- 1 Teaspoon of ground cumin
- 2 Teaspoons of garlic powder
- 1 Pinch of cayenne pepper
- 1 Teaspoon of salt

Directions:

1. Preheat your air fryer to about 390° F
2. In a large wok, fry your ground beef in a little bit of butter and add the taco seasoning; then toss in the tomatoes
3. Put the ground beef into a greased baking tray and add to it the jalapenos and the cheese right on top.
4. Put the baking tray in the basket of the air fryer and close the lid
5. Set the timer to about 20 minutes and the temperature to about 375° F
6. When the timer beeps, remove the baking tray from the air fryer and serve it with the sour cream and a salad of your choice
7. Enjoy!

Nutritional information

- Calories per serving –234.9 calories
- Fat per serving –14.8 grams

- Total Carbs per serving –5.1 grams
- Protein per serving – 22grams

VEGAN LASAGNA

Recipe 25: Vegan Lasagna

(Cooking Time: 35 minutes\ Preparation Time: 15 minutes\ Servings: 3)

- **NOTE:**

There is nothing better than a low carb version of beef lasagna that is made with zucchini and there are no harmful ingredients included at all. If you are going on a special diet, this recipe is absolutely the best for you.

INGREDIENTS:

- 1 Pound of lean ground beef
- 1 and ½ teaspoons of kosher salt
- 1 Teaspoon of olive oil
- ½ Of a large chopped onion
- 3 Minced garlic cloves
- 1 can of 28 oz of crushed tomatoes
- 2 Tablespoons of chopped fresh basil
- 1 Pinch of black pepper
- 2 to 3 medium sliced zucchini

- 1 and ½ cups of part-skim ricotta
- ¼ Cup of Parmigiano Reggiano
- 2 Medium eggs
- 2 Cups of shredded mozzarella cheese

DIRECTIONS:

1. In a medium saucepan and over a medium-high heat, sauté the meat until it becomes brown for about 2 to 3 minutes
2. Season the meat with a little bit of salt and 1 Pinch of pepper
3. Add a little bit of olive oil; add the tomatoes and the basil and let simmer for about 3 minutes
4. Add the meat to your pan and let simmer for about 25 minutes; but make sure not to add water
5. In the meantime, slice the zucchini into quite thick slices and season with salt Remove the zucchini from the sauce and grill it in a preheated grill for about 2 minutes
6. Preheat your air fryer to about 375° F
7. Pat the zucchini dry with paper towels
8. In a deep bowl, combine the ricotta cheese with the parmesan cheese and the egg; In the greased baking tray, lay about ½ cup of your sauce into the bottom of the tray and line the zucchini, then spread about ½ cup of the cheese mixture
9. Spread 1 cup of mozzarella cheese; then repeat the same process until you finish all of your ingredients

10. Make sure the last layer is made of zucchini and mozzarella cheese
11. Cover the lasagna with an aluminum foil tin and put it in the basket of the air fryer; then close the lid
12. Set the timer to about 20 minutes and the temperature to 390° F
13. When the timer beeps, remove the lasagna from the air fryer; then serve and enjoy it!

Nutritional information

- Calories per serving –274 calories
- Fat per serving –13.1 grams
- Total Carbs per serving –11.9 grams
- Protein per serving – 25 grams

AIR FRIED WHITE FISH WITH NUTS

Recipe 26: Air Fried white fish with nuts

(Cooking Time: 15 minutes\ Preparation Time: 5 minutes\ Servings: 4)

- **NOTE:**

With this white fish recipe, you will enjoy one of the most creative dishes ever. This recipe is rich in proteins and low in carbohydrates and it is also gluten-free. If you have had enough of unhealthy food; choose this easy-to make recipe.

INGREDIENTS:

- 2 Fillets of halibut of 6 to 7 oz each 3 T pine nuts
- 2 Tablespoons of Parmesan Cheese
- ¼ Teaspoon of crushed garlic
- 1 Teaspoon of basil pesto
- 1 and ½ tablespoons of mayonnaise

Directions

1. Preheat your air fryer to about 390° F
2. Grease a baking pan that fits your air fryer with cooking spray

3. Finely cut the pine nuts and then mince the garlic cloves.
4. Mix altogether the chopped pine nuts with the Parmesan cheese, the minced garlic, the basil pesto, and the mayonnaise
5. With a rubber scraper; spread the mixture of the crust over the surface of the fish
6. Keep piling the mixture of crust until you finish it all
7. Put the fish in the basket of the greased baking tray and put the tray in the basket of the air fryer
8. Close the lid and set the timer to 15 minutes and the temperature to about 390° F
9. When the timer beeps, remove the fish from the air fryer; then serve and enjoy it with lemon wedges

Nutritional information

- Calories per serving –199.5 calories
- Fat per serving –14 grams
- Total Carbs per serving –4.9 grams
- Protein per serving – 4.1 grams

SHRIMPS WITH OREGANO AND PEPPER FLAKES

Recipe 27: Shrimps with oregano and pepper flakes

(Cooking Time: 15 minutes\ Preparation Time: 18 minutes\ Servings: 3)

- **NOTE:**

A delicious shrimp recipe, simple and rich in fibers; the taste of red pepper flakes adds a spicy taste that you will enjoy. Air fried shrimps are extremely delicious and doesn't need more than a few minutes to be ready. It is a recipe that you can serve in special occasions.

INGREDIENTS:

- 1 Pound of large and deveined peeled shrimp
- 1 Teaspoon of salt
- 1 Teaspoon of dried and crushed red pepper flakes
- 3 Tablespoons of olive oil
- 1 Medium sliced onion
- 1 Can of cubed tomatoes
- 1 Cup of dry white wine
- 3 Finely chopped garlic cloves

- ¼ Teaspoon of dried oregano leaves
- 3 Tablespoon of chopped Italian parsley leaves
- 3 Tablespoon of chopped basil leaves

Directions:

1. Preheat the air fryer to about 365° F
2. In a medium bowl; season the shrimps with 1 pinch of salt and a little bit of red pepper flakes.
3. Grease a baking tray with olive oil and toss the shrimp into your greased baking tray and put it in the basket of the air fryer
4. Close the lid of the air fryer and set the timer to about 3 minutes and the temperature to about 350°F; meanwhile, put the onion in a saucepan and add 2 tablespoons of oil; then sauté for about 2 minutes.
5. Add the wine, the garlic, the oregano and the tomatoes; then let simmer for about 7 minutes
6. Add the shrimps to the tomatoes and add the parsley Add the basil and season with salt
7. Serve and enjoy!

Nutritional information

- Calories per serving –310 calories
- Fat per serving –17.9 grams
- Total Carbs per serving –9.9 grams
- Protein per serving – 24 grams

AIR FRIED SALMON WITH HERBS

Recipe 28: Air fried salmon with herbs

(Cooking Time: 20 minutes\ Preparation Time: 16 minutes\ Servings: 5-6)

- **NOTE:**

Have you ever thought of a simple way to cook salmon with? This salmon recipe is very easy to make and rich in vitamins; you will like its taste and you will get addicted to it.

INGRDIENTS:

- 1/3 Cup of vegetable oil
- 1 and ½ tablespoons of rice vinegar
- 1 Teaspoon of sesame oil
- 1/3 Cup of soy sauce
- ¼ Cup of chopped green onions
- 1 Tablespoon of grated fresh ginger root
- 1 Teaspoon of minced garlic
- 2 Skin removed, salmon fillets

Directions

1. In a large plate or bowl, mix altogether the rice vinegar

with the sesame oil, the vegetable oil, the soy sauce, the ginger, and the garlic.
2. Put the salmon fillets into your prepared marinade and cover it with a lid or a clean cloth; then set it aside for about 18 minutes
3. Preheat your air fryer to a temperature of about 350° F and put the salmon in the basket of the air fryer; then close the lid and set the timer to about 10 minutes
4. When the timer beeps, remove the salmon from the air fryer; then serve and enjoy it with lemon wedges and rice!

Nutritional information

- Calories per serving –233.2 calories
- Fat per serving –11.3 grams
- Total Carbs per serving –1.4 grams
- Protein per serving – 29.1 grams

CODFISH WITH LEMON JUICE

Recipe 29: Codfish with Lemon Juice
(Cooking Time: 25 minutes\ Preparation Time: 15 minutes\ Servings: 3)

- **NOTE:**

If you are looking for a light and crispy recipe; you are not going to find a recipe better than this one. The ingredients of this recipe are affordable and can be found in every house. This recipe is one of the easiest and quickest ways to enjoy the juicy taste of a lunch rich in proteins.

INGREDIENTS:

- 1 Pound of cod fish
- 1 Pinch of salt
- 1 Teaspoon of sugar
- 2 Tablespoons of sesame oil
- 1 Cup of water
- 5 Tablespoons of light soy sauce
- 1 Teaspoon of dark soy sauce

- 5 Rock sugar squares
- 3 Tablespoons of oil
- 5 Slices of ginger
- 1 Thinly sliced onion
- Use coriander for garnish

Directions:

1. Start by washing and patting the cod fish dry with paper towels
2. Season the cod fish 1 pinch of salt and a little bit of sugar
3. Drizzle with sesame oil and set the fish aside for about 15 minutes
4. Preheat the air fryer for about 2 to 3 minutes at about 360° F
5. Put the fish over an aluminum foil tin and put it in the basket of the air fryer.
6. Close the lid of the air fryer and set the timer to 10 minutes; meanwhile, prepare your sauce by pouring about 1 cup of water into a saucepan and let it boil
7. Add the soy sauce and the rock sugar; then let
8. In a small wok, heat the oil and add to it the ginger and the spring onion; then sauté for 2 minutes
9. Remove the cod fish from your air fryer and put it in a serving platter dish
10. Top your swordfish with coriander and serve with the sauce you have prepared
11. Enjoy!

Nutritional information

- Calories per serving –370 calories
- Fat per serving –10.5 grams
- Total Carbs per serving –6.5 grams
- Protein per serving – 37 grams

FISH NUGGETS WITH LEMON JUICE

Recipe 30: Fish Nuggets with lemon juice

(Cooking Time: 10 minutes\ Preparation Time: 5 minutes\ Servings: 2)

- **NOTE:**

Fish Nuggets with lemon juice is a fast lunch recipe that you will heal any illness with its mouthwatering taste. You can serve your fish nuggets with sauce for your choice. A completely healthy recipe you are going to enjoy.

INGREDIENTS

- 1/2 Pound of fish fillet
- 1 Tablespoon of lemon juice
- 3 Tablespoons of milk
- 1 Large egg
- 2 Tablespoons of Dijon mustard
- 2 Tablespoons of yogurt
- 1 Pinch of salt
- 1 Pinch of pepper
- ½ Cup of bread crumbs

Directions

1. Preheat your air fryer to about 390° F
2. Line a baking tray with parchment papers
3. Cut the fish fillets into cubes and drizzle with 2 tablespoons of lemon juice.
4. Sprinkle with a little bit of salt and a little bit of pepper.
5. Into a large bowl, combine the milk, the egg, the mustard and the yogurt.
6. Mix your ingredients very well and add season with a little bit of salt
7. Dip your fish nuggets into the mixture of milk and then into the sauce
8. Remove the nuggets from the sauce and with a fork, drain the nuggets of any exceed of the sauce
9. Coat the nuggets with the breadcrumbs and grease a baking tray with cooking spray
10. Put the nuggets in the baking tray and put in the basket of the air fryer; then close the lid
11. Set the timer to about 10 minutes and the temperature to about 375° F
12. When the timer beeps, remove the fish nuggets from the air fryer; then serve and enjoy with tomato sauce

CHAPTER THREE

SIDE DISHES

RECIPE 31: Potato Beef Croquette

(Cooking Time: 8 minutes\ Preparation Time: 10 minutes\ Servings: 5)

- **NOTE:**

Potato Croquette is a very well-known recipe that no one can ever resist. The taste of the mashed potatoes will make your day better with its taste rich in proteins. You can serve it with mayonnaise and ketchup.

INGREDIENTS:

- 2 Large beaten eggs
- 1 Pound of cooked and drained ground beef
- 2 Cups of cold mashed potatoes
- 1 Medium roughly chopped onion
- ½ Teaspoon of salt
- ¼ Teaspoon of pepper
- 1 Cup of crushed crackers
- 2 Tablespoons of vegetable oil

Directions

1. Crack the eggs into a deep and large bowl
2. Add the potatoes, the beef, the onion, the salt and the pepper; then mix very well
3. Shape your meat into patties or balls and whisk an egg in a small and separate bowl; then dip the meatballs into the egg wash
4. Roll the meatballs into the breadcrumbs
5. Grease a baking tray that fits your air fryer basket; then line the balls into the greased tray and put it in the basket of the air fryer; then close the lid
6. Set the timer to about 8 minutes and the temperature to about 375° F
7. Shake the basket once or twice and when the timer beeps, remove the potato balls from the air fryer; then serve and enjoy it

Nutritional information

- Calories per serving –195.6 calories
- Fat per serving –14.9 grams
- Total Carbs per serving –2.3 grams
- Protein per serving – 11.2 grams

POTATO CHIPS WITH ROSEMARY

Recipe 32: Potato Chips with Rosemary

(Cooking Time: 30 minutes\ Preparation Time: 9 minutes\ Servings: 4)

- **NOTE**

You are hungry and you want to taste a delicious taste of potato chips, but you are afraid of the excessive quantity of oil, then this recipe is yours. Enjoy a crunchy taste of potato chips with a low quantity of oil.

INGREDIENTS:

- 2 Russet Potatoes
- ¼ Cup of olive oil
- ½ Cup of sour cream
- 2 Teaspoons of chopped rosemary
- 1 Tablespoon of roasted Garlic
- 1 Pinch of salt

Directions:

1. Preheat your Air fryer to 390°F.
2. Slice the garlic and put it over an aluminum foil with

the olive oil, the salt and cook the ingredients for about 20 minutes n your air fryer
3. When the timer beeps, remove the ingredients from the air fryer and set it aside
4. Wash your potatoes and peel it; then cut it on a wooden board in a lengthwise method
5. Preheat your air fryer to about 325° F
6. Toss your potato strips into a large bowl and drizzle with olive
7. Put the potato chips into the basket of the air fryer and close the lid
8. Set the timer to about 29 minutes and the temperature to about 330° F
9. When the timer beeps, remove the chips from the air fryer and serve it with the roasted garlic mixed with the rosemary and the sour cream.

Nutritional information

- Calories per serving −160 calories
- Fat per serving −10 grams
- Total Carbs per serving −2.3 grams
- Protein per serving − 3 grams

ZUCCHINI PATTIES WITH PARMESAN CHEESE

Recipe 33: Zucchini Patties with Parmesan cheese
(Cooking Time: 35 minutes\ Preparation Time: 10 minutes\ Servings: 5)

- **NOTE**

Are you struggling to follow a low carb diet and you are eager to eat many types of fried food? This recipe is one of the healthiest and tastiest air fried recipes with zucchini.

INGREDIENTS

- 1 and 1/2 pounds of zucchini
- 1/2 Teaspoon of salt
- 2 Large beaten eggs
- 6 Tablespoons of grated parmesan cheese
- 1 Minced or pressed garlic clove
- ¼ Cup of butter

Directions:

1. Start by combining the coarsely shred zucchini with 1 pinch of salt and 1 pinch of black ground pepper into a large bowl

2. Set the ingredients aside for about 15 minutes; then squeeze it with both your hands in order to press any excess of moisture
3. Add in the eggs, the cheese and the garlic
4. Grease a baking tray that fits your air fryer basket with butter
5. Spoon 1 and ½ tablespoons of the zucchini mixture in your greased baking tray and slightly flatten it; then repeat the same process with the remaining mixture until you finish it all
6. Put the baking tray in the basket of the air fryer and close the lid
7. Set the timer to about 10 minutes and the temperature to about 375° F
8. When the timer beeps, remove the baking tray from the air fryer and set it aside for about 10 minutes to cool; then serve and enjoy it.

Nutritional information

- Calories per serving –199.1 calories
- Fat per serving –16.3 grams
- Total Carbs per serving –6.5 grams
- Protein per serving – 8.2 grams

CHICKEN CHIPOTLE

Recipe 34: Chicken Chipotle

(Cooking Time: 25 minutes\ Preparation Time: 15 minutes\ Servings: 4)

- **NOTE:**

If you are going on a diet and you want an easy recipe as well as a healthy one; then you should make this side dish immediately. Stuffed potatoes are not only very tasty and delicious, but it is also low in carbohydrate and rich in nutrients.

INGREDIENTS:

- 5 to 6 Medium sweet potatoes
- 1 and ½ Pounds of boneless and skinless chicken breasts
- 10 Oz of fresh spinach
- 8 Oz of shredded low-fat cheese of mozzarella
- 2 Tablespoons of olive oil
- 3 Teaspoons of fresh lime juice
- 4 Minced garlic cloves

- 1 Can of chipotle peppers
- 2 Teaspoons of dried oregano
- 1 Teaspoon of cumin
- 2 Teaspoon of chili powder
- 1 Pinch of salt
- 1 Pinch of pepper

Directions:

1. Start by washing the sweet potatoes and poke it with a fork.
2. Season your potatoes with 1 pinch of salt and 1 pinch of pepper; then toss it into the basket of the air fryer and close the lid
3. Set the timer to 15 minutes and the temperature to about 390° F
4. When the timer beeps, remove the potatoes from the air fryer
5. Put the chicken in a greased baking tray and brush it with the lemon juice, the salt and the pepper
6. Put the greased baking tray in the basket of the air fryer and close the lid
7. Set the timer to about 20 minutes and the temperature to about 390° F; meanwhile, mix the lime juice with the olive oil, the garlic, the chipotle peppers and the 3 teaspoons of sauce of adobo. To prepare the sauce mix about 6 chili peppers and add to it 2 finely cut tomatoes; then add a little bit of oil and cook on a low heat
8. Add 1 pinch of salt; then add the oregano, the cumin, the chili powder, the salt and the pepper.
9. Once the timer beeps, remove the chicken from the air fryer and shred it with your hands
10. Cut your potatoes into halves and scrape the potato

flesh from the inside of the potato; but don't remove all the flesh
11. Stuff your potatoes with the shredded chicken, the spinach and the shredded cheese
12. Line the stuffed potatoes halves in a greased baking tray and put it in the basket of the air fryer
13. Set the timer to about 10 minutes and the temperature to about 375° F
14. When the timer beeps, remove the stuffed potatoes from the air fryer; then serve and enjoy it

Nutritional information

- Calories per serving −313.9 calories
- Fat per serving −13.1 grams
- Total Carbs per serving −14 grams
- Protein per serving − 8.2 grams

CAULIFLOWER BITES

Recipe 35: Cauliflower bites

(Cooking Time: 16 minutes\ Preparation Time: 10 minutes\ Servings: 5)

- **NOTE:**

If you want to come up with an innovative and healthy recipe made of vegetables, this recipe is the best to choose. These cauliflower bites are east to make and very delicious; no one can resist its unique taste.

INGRDIENTS:

- 2 Cups of finely, cut cauliflower florets
- 1 Beaten large egg
- 1 Large white of egg
- ½ Cup of minced onion
- 3 Tablespoons of minced fresh parsley
- ½ Cup of grated reduced fat cheddar cheese
- ½ Cup of seasoned breadcrumbs
- 1 Pinch of salt and 1 pinch of pepper
- 2 Tablespoons of cooking spray

Directions:

1. Start by cooking the cauliflower florets by steaming it into 2 cups of cauliflower florets for about 6 minutes
2. Drain the cauliflower very well and pulse the cauliflower into your food processor
3. Preheat your air fryer to about 390° F
4. Grease a baking sheet with cooking spray; then mix all of your ingredients into a large and deep bowl
5. Season with a little bit of salt and 1 pinch of pepper
6. Carefully spoon 1 tablespoon of the mixture into your hands and then start rolling it into balls.
7. Line the balls on top of the cooking sheet and put it in the basket of the air fryer
8. Close the lid of the air fryer and set the timer to 16 minutes and the temperature to about 375° F
9. When the timer beeps, remove the cauliflower bites from the air fryer; then set it aside for about 10 minutes before serving and enjoying it!

Nutritional information

- Calories per serving –148.1 calories
- Fat per serving –5.2 grams
- Total Carbs per serving –12.5 grams
- Protein per serving – 10 grams

CHAPTER FOUR

SNACKS AND APPETIZERS

RECIPE 36: Air Fried Brussels sprouts

(Cooking Time: 20 minutes\ Preparation Time: 15 minutes\ Servings: 3-4)

- **NOTE:**

There are many ways with which we can enjoy the taste of vegetables without steaming it and one of these methods is to air fry Brussels sprouts. If you are eager to try one o of the most delicious crispy veggie recipes; then it is the right time to try Brussels sprouts.

INGREDIENTS:

- 2 Pounds of halved and trimmed Brussels sprouts; remove the outer leaves
- 2 Tablespoons of melted coconut oil
- 1 Teaspoon of dry ketchup spice
- ¾ Teaspoon of fine sea salt
- 1 Pinch of freshly ground black pepper

Directions:

1. Preheat your air fryer to about 390° F; then line a baking

sheet with aluminum foil tin or with parchment paper
2. Trim then ends of the sprouts; then slice it into a lengthwise way
3. Put the sprouts in a large and deep bowl; then drizzle with oil and toss it very well with your hands
4. Add a little bit of salt with Ketchup spice
5. Put the Brussels sprouts above your baking sheet and sprinkle with black pepper
6. Put the baking sheet in the basket of the air fryer and close the lid
7. Set the timer to about 20 minutes and the temperature to 365° F
8. When the timer beeps, remove the Brussels sprouts from the air fryer; then serve and enjoy its crispy taste with salad or rice!

Nutritional information

- Calories per serving –106.3 calories
- Fat per serving –4.5 grams
- Total Carbs per serving –11 grams
- Protein per serving – 5.3 grams

Recipe 37: Falafel
(Cooking Time: 6 minutes\ Preparation Time: 10 minutes\ Servings: 6)

- **NOTE:**

If you want to enjoy the crispiness and the crunchy taste of Falafel; try this recipe; it is healthy, low in carbohydrate and it is perfect to present as a snack. The chickpeas are substituted with cauliflower in this recipe and the addition of almonds adds a unique twist.

INGREDIENTS:

- 1 Cup of raw pureed cauliflower
- ½ Cup of ground slivered almonds
- 1 Tablespoon of ground cumin
- ½ Tablespoon of ground coriander
- 1 Teaspoon of kosher salt
- ½ Teaspoon of cayenne pepper
- 1 Minced garlic clove
- 2 Tablespoons of freshly chopped parsley
- 2 Large beaten eggs
- 3 Tablespoons of coconut flour
- To prepare the Tahini sauce use:
- Tahini sauce:
- 2 Tablespoons of tahini paste
- 4 Tablespoons of water
- 1 Tablespoon of lemon juice
- 1 Minced garlic clove
- 1 Teaspoon of salt

Directions

1. Start by washing the cauliflower; then boil it into about 1 cup of water on a medium heat for 10 minutes
2. Drain the cauliflower and cut it with a knife; then process it with a food processor into fine rice.
3. Grind your almonds with a food processor
4. In a large and deep bowl; combine your ground cauliflower with the almonds; then add the remaining ingredients and mix very well
5. Season your ingredients very well with salt and ground

pepper
6. Grease a baking tray with cooking spray
7. Form small patties by spooning about 1 tablespoon of the mixture until you finish all the mixture
8. Put the baking tray in the basket of your air fryer and close the lid
9. Set the timer to 6 minutes and the heat to 350° F
10. When the timer beeps, remove the baking tray and set it aside for about 10 minutes
11. Serve and enjoy your delicious snack!

Nutritional information

- Calories per serving –281 calories
- Fat per serving –24 grams
- Total Carbs per serving –9.2 grams
- Protein per serving – 8.1 grams

SAMOSA WITH POTATOES AND PEAS

Recipe 38: Samosa with potatoes and peas
(Cooking Time: 30 minutes\ Preparation Time: 15 minutes\ Servings: 5)

- **NOTE:**

This is a light side dish made of vegetables and it is very easy to make. This Samosa recipe only needs a few very affordable ingredients. It is extremely delicious and it can be served with any lunch or dinner.
INGREDIENTS:

- To prepare the Crust of Samosa:
- ½ Cup of Tapioca Flour
- ½ Cup of Almond Flour
- 1 Cup of canned Coconut Milk
- ¼ Teaspoon of salt
- To prepare the Samosa filling:
- 4 Large boiled and mashed russet potatoes
- 1 Cup of boiled peas
- 2 Tablespoons of Grass fed Organic Ghee
- 1 Teaspoon of cumin Seeds

- 1 Medium white onion
- 2 Minced Thai bird chilies
- 1 Minced inch of ginger
- ½ Teaspoon of Kashmiri Chili Powder
- 1 Teaspoon of Coriander Powder
- 1 Teaspoon of Garam Masala
- ½ Teaspoon of salt
- ½ Teaspoon of freshly ground pepper
- ¼ Cup of minced cilantro leaves

Directions

1. Start by making the filling and to do it; boil your potatoes and the peas for about 20 minutes
2. In a medium saucepan; sauté the cumin seeds with the ghee, then chilies, the onions and a little bit of salt
3. Add the ginger; the spices and the mashed potatoes; then sauté for 3 minutes
4. Now time to make the Samosa:
5. In a large and deep bowl, combine the ingredients of Samosa crust in order to form a medium strong batter
6. Pour about 1/3 of your batter into a large non-stick frying pan and cook it for about 2 minutes
7. When you finish cooking the Samosa; put it above a baking tray lined with parchment paper
8. Cut your cooked batter into halves and spoon the prepared filling into the middle of each of the halves of your cooked batter
9. Once you have filled the cooked batter; fold one of its sides on top of the filling; then carefully fold the other side of the sheet of batter onto the other one; you should obtain the shape of a triangle
10. Line the prepared Samosa on the baking sheet and put

in the basket of the air fryer; then close the lid
11. Set the timer to 20 minutes and the temperature to about 350° F
12. When the timer beeps; remove the Samosa from the air fryer; then serve and enjoy it hot

Nutritional information

- Calories per serving −164 calories
- Fat per serving −8 grams
- Total Carbs per serving −7 grams
- Protein per serving − 5.1 grams

TOMATOES WITH HERBS

Recipe 39: Tomatoes with Herbs

(Cooking Time: 20 minutes\ Preparation Time: 5 minutes\ Servings: 2)

- **NOTE:**

This simple recipe made of delicious tomatoes is a succulent snack that you will like. You can make this recipe in a matter of a few minutes; you can even eat it on the go. Fried tomatoes will have a crunchy texture from the outside.

INGREDIENTS

- 4 Tomatoes
- 1 Pinch of salt
- 1 Pinch of pepper
- Herbs
- 2 Tablespoons of cooking spray

Directions:

- Preheat your air fryer to about 325° F
- Wash the tomatoes and cut it into halves
- Turn the tomato on the other side and grease the

- bottom with a drizzle of cooking spray
- Turn all the halves of the tomatoes and season it with a pinch of black pepper, parsley, basil, oregano, thyme, rosemary and sage
- Put the tomato halves in a greased baking tray hat fits your air fryer; then put it in the basket of the air fryer and close the lid and set the timer to about 20 minutes and the temperature to about 325° F
- When the timer beeps, remove the tomatoes from the air fryer; and serve

Nutritional information

- Calories per serving –166.1 calories
- Fat per serving –12.2 grams
- Total Carbs per serving –10.9 grams
- Protein per serving – 2.75 grams

STUFFED PEPPERS WITH GROUND TURKEY

Recipe 40: Stuffed peppers with ground turkey
(Cooking Time: 13 minutes\ Preparation Time: 6 minutes\ Servings: 4-5)

- **NOTE:**

Are you fed up with everyday's junk food you are eating outside? How about making a quick snack in your air fryer? Stuffed peppers are one of the most delicious recipes you will ever taste. These green peppers are stuffed with ground turkey and it can be served with rice.

INGREDIENTS:

- 5 Seeded and cleaned green peppers
- 1 Tablespoon of extra virgin olive oil
- 1/3 Cup of finely chopped onion
- 3 Minced garlic cloves
- ¼ Cup of finely chopped green onion
- 2 Tablespoons of minced green peppers
- 1 Pound of ground turkey
- ½ Ounce can of diced tomatoes
- 1 Tablespoon of parsley

- 1 and ½ teaspoons of Italian seasoning
- 1 Teaspoon of seasoning salt
- ¼ Cup of pizza sauce
- ¼ Cup of shredded mozzarella cheese

Directions:

1. Preheat your air fryer to about 375° F
2. In a medium saucepan, sauté the onion and the garlic with a little bit of olive oil for 2 minutes
3. Add the green onions, the minced green pepper and sauté for about 4 minutes
4. Toss in the turkey meat with the onion, the tomatoes, the tomatoes, the parsley, the Italian seasoning, and season the ingredients with 1 pinch of salt.
5. Mix very well and cook for about 5 minutes
6. Stuff the mixture you have prepared into the green peppers
7. Line the green stuffed peppers into a greased baking tray and put it in the instant fryer basket; then close the lid
8. Set the timer to about 8 minutes and the temperature to about 350° F
9. When the timer beeps; remove the peppers from the air fryer; then serve and enjoy it with pizza sauce

Nutritional information

- Calories per serving –297.8 calories
- Fat per serving –16.2 grams
- Total Carbs per serving –11.7 grams
- Protein per serving – 27.8 grams

CHAPTER FIVE

DESSERT RECIPES

RECIPE 41: Chocolate Fondant

(Cooking Time: 10 minutes\ Preparation Time: 5 minutes\ Servings: 5)

- **NOTE:**

Who amongst us doesn't like eating Chocolate fondants, but we are always worried about the carbohydrates it provides. Thus, we are offering you a recipe that will let you enjoy the world of chocolate and its irresistible taste in this low carb dessert recipe.

INGREDIENTS

- 2Tablespoons of self Raising Flour
- 4Tablespoons of Caster Sugar
- 1 Cup of Dark Chocolate
- 1 Cup of butter
- 1 Orange; both the rind and the juice
- 2 Large eggs

Directions:

1. Preheat your air fryer to about 360° F
2. Grease 4 steel or heat proof ramekins.
3. Start by melting the chocolate and the butter into a heat proof pan filled with water over a medium-high heat
4. In a small bowl, crack the eggs and beat with it the sugar
5. Remove the chocolate from the heat and add to it the mixture of the sugar and the eggs; then whisk very well.
6. Add the flour and mix the ingredients very well; then fill the ramekins, each with about 2/3 full with the mixture; then line the ramekins in the basket of the air fryer and close the lid
7. Set the timer to about 11 minutes and the temperature to 350°F
8. When the timer beeps, remove the ramekins from the air fryer and set it aside to cool for about 10 minutes; then put it over a serving dish and poke your fondant with a knife in the middle
9. Serve and enjoy with caramel sauce!

Nutritional information

- Calories per serving −235.5 calories
- Fat per serving −22.5 grams
- Total Carbs per serving −10.5 grams
- Protein per serving − 4.6 grams

MACADAMIA COOKIES

Recipe 42: Macadamia cookies

(Cooking Time: 17 minutes\ Preparation Time: 10 minutes\ Servings: 7)

- **NOTE:**

The combination of the almond butter to the macadamia adds a rich flavor to the cookies and grants you a chewy and nutty taste. You will enjoy the crispiness of these cookies, besides, this recipe is low in carb and it is perfect for all kinds of diets.

INGREDIENTS

- ½ Cup of melted butter
- 2 Tablespoons of almond butter
- 1 Large egg
- 1 and ½ cups of almond flour
- 2 Tablespoons of unsweetened cocoa powder
- ½ Cup of granulated erythritol sweetener
- 1 Teaspoon of vanilla extract
- ½ Teaspoon of baking soda
- ¼ Cup of chopped macadamia nuts
- 1 Pinch of salt

Directions

1. Preheat your air fryer to about 365° F
2. In a large and deep bowl; mix your ingredients and whisk it very well until you obtain firm dough
3. Prepare a cookie sheet by lining it with a parchment paper; then grease it with cooking spray
4. Make the shape of cookies; then line the cookies on the baking sheet; then it in the basket of the air fryer and close the lid
5. Set the timer to about 17 minutes and the temperature to about 350° F
6. When the timer beeps, remove the cookies from the air fryer and set it aside for about 10minutes; then serve and enjoy!

Nutritional information

- Calories per serving –136 calories
- Fat per serving –13.1 grams
- Total Carbs per serving –4.5 grams
- Protein per serving – 3.1 grams

MACAROONS WITH PISTACHIO TOPPING

Recipe 43: Macaroons with Pistachio topping

(Cooking Time: 15 minutes\ Preparation Time: 90 minutes\ Servings: 10)

- **NOTE:**

Macaroons make a delicious and beautifully presented dessert that is worth making. You will love the taste of Pistachio macaroons and its light texture. It is a perfect recipe to serve with lemonade.

INGREDIENTS

To make the shells:

- 2 Egg white large egg whites
- ½ Oz of erythritol
- 3 oz of blanched almonds
- ½ Teaspoons of matcha tea powder
- 5 Oz of powdered erythritol
- To make the topping of the pistachios
- 1 and ½ oz of unsalted pistachios
- 1/8 Teaspoon of stevia extract
- ½ Teaspoon of vanilla extract

- 2/3 oz of unsalted butter

Directions

1. Start by making the shells
2. Preheat your air fryer to about 325° F and lien a baking sheet with a parchment paper
3. Ground the toasted almonds; then pulse it with a food processor for about 40 seconds
4. Add the erythritol and keep processing until you obtain fine almond flour by processing for 1 additional minute and with a processor,
5. Beat in the eggs and mix all of the ingredients together until you get a fluffy mixture
6. Add the powder of matcha and when the batter gets a green color; add the about 1/3 of your mixture of erythritol with the almond flour and mix on a very low speed
7. With a spatula, add mix your ingredients very well; then stir in the rest of the erythritol mixture; then transfer your mixture very well to a plastic bag for pastry; then cut the tip into a hole of ½ inch; then start piping the cookies on the baking pan lined with the parchment paper
8. Set the cookies aside to dry for about 50 minutes
9. Put the baking tray in the air fryer basket and close the lid
10. Set the timer to about 15 minutes and the temperature to about 325° F
11. When the timer beeps, remove the cookies from the air fryer and set it aside to cool for 10 minute: meanwhile prepare the pistachio topping by grounding the pistachio with the erythritol.

12. With an electric mixer, combine the butter with the stevia very well; then add the pistachio mixture and add the extract of the vanilla
13. Line your pistachio macaroons on a serving platter and fill each with a spoon of the cream of the pistachio; then cover the shell with another shell with a similar size.
14. Set the macaroons in the refrigerator for about 30 minutes; then serve and enjoy!

Nutritional information

- Calories per serving −76 calories
- Fat per serving −6.7 grams
- Total Carbs per serving −2.3 grams
- Protein per serving − 2.2 grams

CHOCOLATE BARS

Recipe 44: Chocolate Bars
(Cooking Time: 30 minutes\ Preparation Time: 20 minutes\ Servings: 12)

- **NOTE:**

Chocolate bars recipe is an easy dessert to make; it is simple; delicious and low n carbohydrates. You can enjoy making chocolate bars with or without the chocolate coating anytime of the day.

INGREDIENTS
Ingredients to prepare the bars

- 2 Tablespoons of coconut oil
- ¾ Cup of creamy almond butter
- ¾ Cup of unsweetened almond milk
- 2 Cups of low carb baking mix (Made of ¼ cup of oat fiber+ ¼ Cup of coconut flour+ ¼ cup ofo flax meal)
- ¼ Cup of almond flour
- 1 Large egg
- ½ Teaspoon of baking soda
- ½ Cup of chopped walnuts

- 2 Teaspoons of vanilla extract
- 1 Teaspoon of stevia
- 2 Tablespoons of erythritol
- For the chocolate topping:
- 4 Oz of unsweetened baking chocolate
- ¼ Cup of coconut oil
- 1 Teaspoon of stevia
- ¼ Cup of powdered erythritol
- ⅛ Teaspoon of salt
- 1 Teaspoon of vanilla extract
- ½ Cup of slivered almonds for garnishing

Directions

1. Start by mixing the ingredients of the bars into a large and deep mixing bowl; then when it starts being a lit bit sticky; press your dough into a greased baking tray
2. Preheat your air fryer to about 350° F
3. Line the cookies on the greased baking tray; then put the tray in the basket of the air fryer and close the lid
4. Set the timer to about 25 minutes and bake your cookies
5. When the timer beeps, remove the cookies from the air fryer and set it aside for about 10 minutes; meanwhile; melt the chocolate in your microwave in a heat-proof bowl and add to it the rest of the topping ingredients
6. Add the vanilla by the end
7. Spoon your chocolate over the cooked bars and top it with your almonds; then set aside for about 25 minutes in the refrigerator
8. Serve and enjoy!

Nutritional information

- Calories per serving –161.1 calories
- Fat per serving –13.1 grams
- Total Carbs per serving –7.9 grams
- Protein per serving – 5.1 grams

ORANGE CAKE

Recipe 45: Orange Cake

(Cooking Time: 25 minutes\ Preparation Time: 40 minutes\ Servings: 5)

- **NOTE:**

We are always looking for a sweet dessert to enjoy in our evenings with the family and friends; but we find ourselves stuck as we can't find a sugar-free dessert. This recipe will be your perfect choice as it uses natural ingredients that won't endanger your health; you are going to enjoy it.

INGREDIENTS:

- 2 Quartered orange
- 6 Large eggs
- 9 Oz of almond flour
- 1 Teaspoon of baking powder
- 3 Tablespoons of granulated maple syrup
- 1 Teaspoon of vanilla
- ¼ Teaspoon of salt

Directions:

1. Start by putting the oranges into a large saucepan and add to it about ½ cup of water
2. Let the ingredients simmer into the water over a medium-low heat for about 30 minutes
3. Remove the oranges from the saucepan; then set it aside to cool
4. Preheat your air fryer to about 375° F
5. Grease a spring baking tray with a little bit of butter; then sprinkle a little bit of flour
6. Cut the oranges and blend the pieces with eggs into a blender
7. In a deep and large bowl, combine the almonds with the sugar and the baking powder; then mix very well
8. Add the almond flour and the orange mixture; then whisk very well
9. Pour the batter into the baking tray and put it in the basket of the air fryer; then close the lid and set the timer to about 25 to 30 minutes and the temperature to about 350° F
10. When the timer beeps, remove the cake from the air fryer and set it aside to cool for 5 minutes; then serve and enjoy it!

Nutritional information

- Calories per serving –178.1 calories
- Fat per serving –1.4 grams
- Total Carbs per serving –13.1 grams
- Protein per serving – 3.4 grams

ALMOND SEMOLINA CAKE

Recipe 46: Almond Semolina cake

(Cooking Time: 45 minutes\ Preparation Time: 15 minutes\ Servings: 7)

- **NOTE:**

This semolina cake recipe is incredibly delicious and very unique with its crumbly texture. Making semolina cake will make you change your mind about the recipes you should make. The ingredients of semolina cake are affordable and healthy as well as rich in fibres and nutrients.

INGREDIENTS:

- ½ Cup and 2 tablespoons of unsalted butter
- 1 Cup of sugar
- 1 Cup of plain yogurt
- 1 Cup of fine semolina
- 1 Cup of coarse semolina
- 1/3 Cup of milk
- 1 Teaspoon of baking powder
- ¼ Cup of sweetened shredded coconut

- ¼ Cup of shaved almonds
- To make the cinnamon simple syrup:
- 1 and ½ cup of sugar
- 1 and ¾ cup of water
- 1 Stick of cinnamon
- ¼ Teaspoon of lemon juice

Directions:

1. Preheat your air fryer to about of 350° F
2. In a small and deep bowl; melt the butter into a microwave
3. Mix the yogurt and the sugar into a large bowl; then add the baking powder and whisk the ingredients altogether very well
4. Add the baking powder; the semolina and the milk; then add the butter and mix your ingredients
5. Grease a baking tray that fits your air fryer basket; then pour the batter into the tray and put the tray into the basket of the air fryer and close the lid
6. Set the timer to about 35 to 40 minutes and the temperature to 350° F; meanwhile; prepare the syrup by mixing the sugar; the water and the cinnamon stick; then cook for about 10 minutes on a medium high heat
7. When the timer beeps, carefully remove the semolina tray and set it aside to cool for 15 minutes
8. Pour the syrup over the semolina and set it aside for about 1 hour to absorb the syrup
9. Top with shredded coconuts; then slice the semolina; serve and enjoy!

Nutritional information

- Calories per serving –189.3 calories
- Fat per serving –9.8 grams
- Total Carbs per serving –12.8 grams
- Protein per serving – 5.9 grams

CRISPY LOW CARB GLAZED PASTRY DESSERT

Recipe 47: Crispy Low carb glazed pastry dessert
(Cooking Time: 35 minutes\ Preparation Time: 90 minutes\ Servings: 12)

- **NOTE:**

When you make this crispy and healthy dessert recipe; you will love it and you will get addicted to it. The crispy taste with the glaze is really mouthwatering and perfect to serve in any occasion. What a simple and succulent dessert!

INGREDIENTS:

- 1 Package of 1 pound Phyllo Dough
- 1 Cup of Almonds
- 1 Tablespoon of Coconut Sugar
- 1 Tablespoon of Xylitol
- ½ Teaspoon of cinnamon
- 1 Pinch of salt
- ½ Cup of unsalted Butter
- To make the glaze:

- ¾ cups of water
- ¾ cup of Honey
- 1 tablespoon of cinnamon
- 1 Teaspoon of Lemon Juice

Directions:

1. Pulse the almonds until you obtain a fine meal. Then add the sweeteners, the cinnamon and the salt; then mix very well.
2. Place the dough over a hard and clean work surface; then take out about 3 sheets and lay it right in front of you
3. Make sure to keep your dough moist with a damp paper
4. With a rod or 2 and ½ inches diameter; lay the dough on top and sprinkle the mixture of the almond right on top of all the dough
5. Make sure to leave an inch right on the edge of the bottom part of your pastry dough
6. Try using about 4 tablespoons of the mixture of almonds per each pastry roll
7. Rub about 2 tablespoons of butter over the pastry dough; and distribute it evenly on the dough
8. Roll the dough over the almonds; then gently scrunch the ends and the middle in order to make the dough a little bit wrinkly
9. Carefully, pull the dough gently out of the rod and put it in a greased baking tray
10. Brush the top of your rolls generously with butter.
11. Repeat the same process until you finish the quantity of dough
12. Sprinkle the top of the dough with a little bit of almond and lay it all in the greased baking tray; then put the

tray in the basket of the air fryer and close the lid
13. Set the timer to 35 minutes and the temperature to about 365° F; in the mean time; prepare the glaze by combining all of its ingredients into a saucepan and let it boil for about 15 minutes over a medium heat
14. When the timer beeps; remove the pastry from the air fryer and drizzle the syrup over it while it is still hot
15. Let the pastry cool for about 15 minutes; then serve and enjoy it!

Nutritional information

- Calories per serving –101 calories
- Fat per serving –5.01 grams
- Total Carbs per serving –13 grams
- Protein per serving – 1.2 grams

CRUNCHY WALNUT COOKIES

Recipe 48: Crunchy Walnut cookies

(Cooking Time: 21 minutes\ Preparation Time: 15 minutes\ Servings: 9-10)

- **NOTE:**

These Walnut Cookies you are going to make you feel happy with the mixture of tastes it provides you with. You will enjoy each bite of the crunchy walnut cookies with the taste of the cinnamon, pistachio and lemon juice. Serve it anytime and enjoy its delicious taste.

INGREDIENTS:

- To make the pastry dough:
- 3 Oz of softened cream cheese
- 5 Oz of softened stick butter
- 1 Cup of Blend Baking Mix made of even quantities of ground flax, coconut flour and almond flour
- For the filling of Nut:
- ½ Cup of walnuts
- ¼ Cup of pistachios
- ½ Teaspoon of cinnamon

- For the Syrup:
- ½ Cup of erythritol
- 1 Tablespoon of water
- 3 Pieces of lemon zest of 1 inch each
- 1 Stick of cinnamon
- 3 Teaspoons of honey

Directions

1. Preheat your air fryer to about 350°
2. Grease a baking muffin tin with a little bit of cooking spray
3. In a large bowl; combine all of your dough ingredients in a medium and whisk it with a wooden spoon.
4. Split the pieces of dough into about 24 parts and press each portion into each of the muffin holes (You can use a measuring spoon to do this)
5. Put the baking tin in the basket of the air fryer and close the lid
6. Set the timer to about 21 minutes and the temperature to 350° F
7. In the mean time, prepare the syrup by mixing the water with the sweetener; then lemon zest and the cinnamon stick and let boil for about 5 minutes over a medium low heat
8. When the timer beeps, remove the baking tin from the air fryer and pour the syrup over it
9. Let your cookies cool for 10 minutes; then serve and enjoy it!

Nutritional information

- Calories per serving –138.1 calories
- Fat per serving –10.1 grams

- Total Carbs per serving –10.7 grams
- Protein per serving – 3.2 grams

RASPBERRY COCONUT BALLS

Recipe 49: Raspberry coconut balls

(Cooking Time: 10 minutes\ Preparation Time: 8 minutes\ Servings: 9)

- **NOTE:**

You don't need complicated ingredients to make this dessert recipe. With a few ingredients, you will get this recipe ready in a very short time. Each ball will provide you with a great amount of proteins and fibers. And if you are following a strict diet; you will be able to eat this dessert too because it is low in carbohydrates

INGREDIENTS:

- ¼ Cup of coconut flour
- ¼ Cup of cocoa powder
- ¼ Teaspoon of salt
- ¼ Teaspoon of baking powder
- ½ Cup of Swerve
- 3 Large eggs
- ¼ Cup of melted coconut oil
- 10 Drops of chocolate raspberry flavoring

- ¼ Cup of water or almond milk

To coat the balls:

- ¼ Cup of coconut oil
- ¼ Cup of cocoa powder
- 6 Teaspoons of stevia
- 5 Drops of chocolate raspberry flavoring

Directions:

1. In a medium large bowl, combine all of your dry ingredients together and mix very well
2. Crack in the eggs with the flavoring and the oil
3. Add the almond milk if your batter has become very thick.
4. Make balls out of the dough; then grease a muffin tin with cooking spray
5. Put the dough balls in the muffin tin holes and spoon the butter on top of each of the balls
6. Preheat your air fryer to about 350° F
7. Put the baking tin in the basket of the air fryer and close the lid
8. Set the timer for about 6 to 7 minutes
9. When the timer beeps, remove the muffin tins from the air fryer and set it aside for about 10 minutes
10. Prepare the dipping by mixing the cocoa powder with the stevia and the raspberry flavor
11. Dip the balls in the flavoring and set it aside to cool for 15 minutes
12. Serve and enjoy!

Nutritional information

- Calories per serving –236.1 calories
- Fat per serving –21 grams
- Total Carbs per serving –4.9 grams
- Protein per serving – 5 grams

GLAZED DONUTS

Recipe 50: Glazed Donuts

(Cooking Time: 35 minutes\ Preparation Time: 20 minutes\ Servings: 10)

- **NOTE:**

Have you ever tried this moist donut recipe? If not, you should make these glazed donuts wit crumbs. It is a simple recipe that only needs a few and very affordable ingredients.

INGREDIENTS:

- To make the donuts:
- 2 Tablespoons of softened butter
- ¼ Cup of sour cream
- 2 tbsp Trim Healthy Mama Gentle Sweet (or my combo of xylitol, erythritol, and stevia)
- ¼ Cup of almond flour
- ¼ Cup of coconut flour+ ground flax
- 1 Large egg
- 1 Teaspoon of vanilla
- ½ Teaspoon of baking powder
- 1 Pinch of salt

- For the topping of crumb:
- ½ Cup of almond flour
- 2 Teaspoon of coconut flour
- 3 Tablespoon of softened butter
- 3 Tablespoons of sweetener
- To make the glaze:
- 2 Tablespoons of butter
- ½ Cup of sweetener

Directions:

1. Preheat your air fryer to about 350°F
2. In a large bowl; combine your ingredient altogether to form a batter; then grease a muffin tin with cooking spray
3. Divide your batter between the muffin holes; meanwhile, combine the ingredients of the crumbs in a bowl and mix it very well
4. Spread the crumbs with your hands over your already prepared donut batter
5. Put the baking tray in the basket of your air fryer and close the lid
6. Set the timer for 20 minutes and the temperature to about 365° F; in the meantime; prepare your glaze in a medium saucepan
7. Melt your butter in the saucepan and add the sweetener to it; then let cook on a low heat for about 10 minutes
8. When the timer beeps, remove the muffin tin from the Air fryer and set it aside to cool for about 5 minutes over a wire rack
9. Pour the glaze over your donuts; then repeat the same

       process until you finish all the donuts
    10. Set the ingredients aside for the glaze to thicken for about 5 minutes
    11. Serve and enjoy!

Nutritional information

- Calories per serving –120 calories
- Fat per serving –11.6 grams
- Total Carbs per serving –2.3 grams
- Protein per serving – 2.2 grams

CHAPTER SIX

RECIPE INDEX

RECIPE 1: Blueberry oats Breakfast casserole
Recipe 2: Cinnamon Almond Toast
Recipe 3: Gluten Free Ham Frittata
Recipe 4: Granola with chocolate and Hazelnuts
Recipe 5: Avocado Egg Boats
Recipe 6: Cloud pancakes with scallions
Recipe 7: Whole wheat Burritos
Recipe 8: Air Fried Quiche muffins
Recipe 9: Air Fried pancakes
Recipe 10: Air Fried pancakes
Recipe 11: Chicken with garlic and olives
Recipe 12: Crispy Chicken Livers
Recipe 13: Chicken with broccoli and sesame
Recipe 14: Chicken with sesame and Orange sauce
Recipe 15: Chicken with Parmesan cheese
Recipe 16: Turkey breast with thyme and sage
Recipe 17: Chicken Pizza
Recipe 18: Almond Crusted Chicken
Recipe 19: Pistachio stuffed chicken
Recipe 20: Chicken balls with tomato sauce
Recipe 21: Beef curry

Recipe 22: Beef Rouladen
Recipe 23: Beef meat Jerky
Recipe 24: Beef Casserole with Cheese
Recipe 25: Vegan Lasagna
Recipe 26: Air Fried white fish with nuts
Recipe 27: Shrimps with oregano and pepper flakes
Recipe 28: Air fried salmon with herbs
Recipe 29: Codfish with Lemon Juice
Recipe 30: Fish Nuggets with lemon juice
Recipe 31: Potato Beef Croquette
Recipe 32: Potato Chips with Rosemary
Recipe 33: Zucchini Patties with Parmesan cheese
Recipe 34: Chicken Chipotle
Recipe 35: Cauliflower bites
Recipe 36: Air Fried Brussels sprouts
Recipe 37: Falafel
Recipe 38: Samosa with potatoes and peas
Recipe 39: Tomatoes with Herbs
Recipe 40: Stuffed peppers
Recipe 41: Chocolate Fondant
Recipe 42: Macadamia cookies
Recipe 43: Macaroons with Pistachio topping
Recipe 44: Chocolate Bars
Recipe 45: Orange Cake
Recipe 46: Almond Semolina cake
Recipe 47: Crispy Low carb glazed pastry dessert
Recipe 48: Crunchy Walnut cookies
Recipe 49: Raspberry coconut balls
Recipe 50: Glazed Donuts

CHAPTER SEVEN

CONCLUSION

Together To Make our Life Better with this book:
"RACE TO TASTE THE HEALTHIEST AIR FRIED RECIPES"
Helps you learn and enjoy the most delicious recipes you can ever taste.

The majority of the people around the globe want to enjoy the taste of fried food, but they keep being concerned because of the high count of carbohydrates they would consume. All the air fried recipes in this book are healthy with affordable ingredients. With this air fried recipes; all your worries about saturated fats and harmful effects will disappear because scientific studies have proved that the included low-carb air fried recipes are 100% healthy for all diets. You will be surprised by the astonishing taste and the mouthwatering taste.

THANK YOU FOR READING THIS BOOK

We are very proud and happy to offer you this Air Fried Low Carb Recipe Book where you can learn everything related to cooking using an air fryer, even if it is your first time. You will enjoy this innovative cooking book with its versatile recipes that vary from breakfast recipes to Lunch recipes and more.

ALSO BY FRANCESCA BONHEUR

Air Fryer Cookbook: Quick and Easy Low Carb Air Fryer Chicken Recipes

Ketogenic Cookbook: Reset your metabolism with these easy Beef recipes

Ketogenic Cookbook: Reset your metabolism with these easy, healthy and delicious ketogenic Chicken recipes

Ketogenic Cookbook: Low carb, delicious and healthy ketogenic slow cooker recipes to reset your metabolism and kick start your keto diet to lose fat

Ketogenic Cookbook: Reset Your Metabolism With these Easy, Healthy and Delicious Ketogenic and Pressure Cooker Vegan Recipes

ketogenic cookbook: A step by step beginners diet plan to reset your metabolism with these easy, healthy and delicious low carb meals

ABOUT THE AUTHOR

Francesca Bonheur is a thirty-five year old traveler, successful chef, and passionate nutritionist, born in her mother's hometown of Toulouse, France. At a very young age, Francesca noticed how people can be brought together by food, and she began paying close attention to her parents while they were preparing meals. It was at the age of two that Francesca began to join her parents in the kitchen on a daily basis, assisting however she was able. Before the age of five, she could prepare many family meals almost entirely by herself. Throughout her developmental years, Francesca was obsessed with improving her knowledge of ingredients and techniques, and so she would spend much of her free time reading cookbooks from cover to cover, and visiting the chefs who worked at successful restaurants in Toulouse. After graduating high school, Francesca left home to pursue a professional career in the culinary arts. She apprenticed and worked with several French chefs over a period of fifteen years before making her way to Italy to discover her Italian roots on her Father's side. Now Francesca's cooking style is a combination of her years spent in the best restaurants in Italy and France, her knowledge of French culinary technique, and her parent's French and Italian roots. At age thirty-two, Francesca decided to take a break from the discipline that is often found in restaurant kitchens, and began to travel. Today, Francesca can usually be found traveling between in Naples, Italy, and her hometown of Toulouse, but can occasionally be found on other continents as well, creating diet plans and cookbooks that pay homage to rich and savoury flavours, without breaking calorie count.

Made in the USA
Columbia, SC
04 January 2021